THOMAS JEFFERSON

1743-1826

Chronology–Documents–Bibliographical Aids

Edited by
ARTHUR BISHOP

Series Editor
HOWARD F. BREMER

71-2011

1971
OCEANA PUBLICATIONS, INC.
Dobbs Ferry, New York

Library of Congress Catalog Card Number: 70-140619

International Standard Book Number: 0-379-12082-8

Manufactured in the United States of America

CONTENTS

BIBLIOGRAPHICAL AIDS

EDITOR'S FOREWORD

This series is a research tool compiled primarily for the student. Each volume contains a chronology of the president, a selection of his speeches and papers, and an annotated bibliography.

The editor has made every effort to cite accurate dates in the chronology through reference to diaries, letters, documents, and other sources. Sometimes, however, even original materials give conflicting dates, and thus many cannot be established with absolute certainty. Some errors have become enshrined as truth simply through repetition by respected scholars over the years. In these situations, the more plausible date, with the help of recent scholarship, has been selected. Should any item in the chronology differ with other authorities, original sources of the works of such outstanding scholars as biographer-historian Dumas Malone may perhaps resolve the conflict.

The editor has tried to be objective and not make judgments on the significance of events or documents. But obviously the very selection of events and papers excludes others, and that is a judgment. But it is a judgment tempered by an attempt to be impartial.

Whenever possible, the titles annotated in the bibliography are respected works available in paperback editions.

Documents in this volume have been taken from Messages and Papers of the President, Vol. 3 Jefferson, James D. Richardson, ed. (Washington, 1897); Select Documents Illustrative of the History of the United States, 1776-1861, William MacDonald, ed. (New York and London, 1898); and The Life of Thomas Jefferson, 3 vols. Henry S. Randall (New York 1858).

CHRONOLOGY

YOUTH

1743

April 13
(April 2,
Old Style)

Born at Shadwell, his father's estate in Albemarle County, Virginia, the third child and first son of Peter and Jane Randolph Jefferson. They had ten children in all: six daughters and four sons.

1745

After the death of William Randolph, the Jeffersons moved into his estate, Tuckahoe, 50 miles from Shadwell, to care for his son Thomas Mann ("Tuckahoe Tom") Randolph. Thomas began studying under his cousin's tutor at the age of five.

1751

First map of the colony of Virginia, partly surveyed and drawn by Peter Jefferson and Thomas Fry, published in London.

1752

Jefferson family returned to Shadwell, and Thomas began attending Rev. William Douglas' Latin school, where he also studied Greek and French.
Peter Jefferson appointed Colonel of the county, a post combining command of the militia and civil administration.

1754

Peter Jefferson chosen to represent Albemarle in the Virginia House of Burgesses.

1757

August 17

Peter Jefferson died at age 49, leaving Thomas head of the family at 14. Soon thereafter, he enrolled in a school run by Rev. James Maury, a scholar who had graduated from the College of William and Mary in Williamsburg.

STUDENT

1760

March   Entered the College of William and Mary as an advanced student although only 17. Formed a close friendship with Patrick Henry, who was in Williamsburg to obtain a lawyer's license. They had met the previous Christmas.

1762

March   Graduated from William and Mary.

April 25   Began to study law under George Wythe, a leading lawyer in Williamsburg.

1763

Received--and accepted--an invitation to join a group of pre-eminent intellectuals (Governor Francis Fauquier, George Wythe, and William Small) which met for dinner and discussion periodically.

1764

Began recording comments upon his reading of Greek, Latin, and English literature in a "commonplace" book. Over the next few years, he started another on equity law and another on theories of government.

1765

May 30   Heard Patrick Henry deliver his "If this be treason, make the most of it," speech in the House of Burgesses.

July 20   Martha Jefferson, his sister, married Dabney Carr.

October 1   Oldest and favorite sister, Jane, died at age 25.

1766

Spring   Began his garden book, the first of many pocket ac-
                counts of his farm, financial, and other transactions.

May   Left Virginia for the first time to go to New York, stop-
                ping at Annapolis and Philadelphia on the way.

YOUNG LAWYER

1767

February 12   Received his first legal fee for handling a case in the
                General Court.

1768

May 18   Arranged to have the top of a mountain south of the
                Rivanna River near Shadwell leveled--the start of Mon-
                ticello.

1769

April 3   Left Shadwell to attend his first session of the House
                of Burgesses representing Albemarle County--his first
                political office.

May 17   Norborne Berkeley, Baron of Botetourt, the new Gov-
                ernor, dissolved the House immediately after hearing
                the Burgess' "humble petition" to the King concerning
                taxation and other grievances read on the floor.

May 18   Met with other members of the disbanded House in the
                Raleigh Tavern and formed an association to protect
                the colony's interests.

Summer   Ordered 14 books, all on the theory of government in-
                stead of law and literature as in the past.

1771

February 1   Shadwell burned, destroying most of his books and pa-
                pers.

November 26   Moved into a 20-foot square, one-room "outchamber"
                     at Monticello while the main house was being built.

1772

January 1   Married Martha Wayles Skelton, the widow of his friend
                     Bathurst Skelton, who had died three years earlier.
                     She was 23; he was 28.

September 27   First child, Martha Washington Jefferson, born at Mon-
                     ticello.

RADICAL LEADER

1773

March 12   Dabney Carr introduced a resolution, written by Jef-
                     ferson, in the House to establish a permanent Commit-
                     tee of Correspondence. The new Governor, Lord Dun-
                     more, immediately dissolved the House.

March 13   Met with other members of the Committee of Corre-
                     spondence to prepare a circular letter to the other
                     colonies asking them to appoint correspondents and
                     proposing an annual meeting of all the colonies.

May 16   Dabney Carr died, leaving Martha with six children.
                     They all moved into Monticello, where Carr was buried.

May 30   Received word that John Wayles, his wife's father, had
                     died. He left her enough slaves and land to double
                     Jefferson's holdings, but also 3,750 pounds of debts
                     which, when they were finally paid off in 1792, took
                     nearly half of Jefferson's property.

July 15   Advertised 5,320 acres of land for sale--the first of
                     several sales over the years to pay his father-in-law's
                     debts.

October   Appointed Surveyor of Albemarle County.

1774

April 3   Second child, second daughter, born at Monticello and
               named Jane Randolph Jefferson, after her grandmother.

May 26   Governor Dunmore again dissolved the House the day
               after introduction of a resolution proposing a day of fast-
               ing to protest the closing of the port of Boston.

May 27   Met with 80 other Burgesses to form a permanent as-
               sociation and ask the Committee of Correspondence to
               propose annual meetings with the other colonies to dis-
               cuss common problems.

June 1   Day of fasting throughout Virginia.

July 26   A meeting in Albemarle adopted Jefferson's instructions
               for delegates to the First Virginia Convention (The Al-
               bemarle Resolutions) on August 1 and elected Jefferson
               one of the delegation. He became ill on the way to Wil-
               liamsburg and returned home.

August   Payton Randolph, his cousin and chairman of the Con-
               vention, placed a copy of Jefferson's appeal to George III
               to redress the colonies' grievances before the meeting.
               The Convention adopted a more moderate appeal, but
               Jefferson's was printed in Williamsburg during the month
               and later in England as "A Summary View of the rights
               of British America."

August 11   Retired from his law practice to devote more time to
               politica after turning his clients over to Edmond Ran-
               dolph, a cousin, in return for one-third the fees.

1775

January   Elected to the Albemarle Committee of Safety and be-
               came its chairman.

March 20   Attended the Second Virginia Convention and heard Pat-
               rick Henry give his "Give me liberty or give me death"

speech on March 23. A few days later, Jefferson was appointed to a committee to plan for arming and training a militia and elected an alternate to the Second Continental Congress.

June 1	Attended a special session of the House of Burgesses called to consider Lord North's conciliatory proposals of February 27, 1775.
June 8	Governor Dunmore and his family fled to <u>Fowey</u>, a British warship anchored off Yorktown, ending British rule in Virginia for all time.
June 10	Jefferson's reply to Lord North's conciliatory proposals read in the House of Burgesses, which adopted it.
June 11	Left Williamsburg to attend the Second Continental Congress in place of Payton Randolph, who remained to help form and head the new government of Virginia.
June 20	Arrived in Philadelphia and began attending Congress the next day. Only John Jay of New York was a younger delegate than Jefferson.
June 26	Added to a committee preparing "An Address on the Causes of Taking up Arms." John Dickinson wrote it all, except for Jefferson's final four paragraphs, and Congress accepted it on July 6.
July 31	Congress adopted Jefferson's reply to Lord North's conciliatory proposals, which called for a complete redress of grievances or war.
August 1	Congress adjourned and Jefferson left Philadelphia. Later in the month he attended another Virginia Convention in Richmond and was appointed to a seven-man delegation to the next Continental Congress in September.

September	Jane Randolph Jefferson, his second child and second daughter, died.
September 26	Appointed commander of the Albemarle militia.
September 30	Arrived in Philadelphia to attend Congress.
Fall	Governor Dunmore established a base at Norfolk, raised a loyalist army, promised freedom to any Negro who joined him, and began raiding in Virginia.
November 9	Congress learned that George III had refused to receive John Dickinson's petition of July 8 and had declared the colonies in open rebellion on August 23.
December 28	Received permission to leave Congress because of his mother's illness.

1776

January 20	Thomas Paine's <u>Common Sense</u> published.
March 31	His mother, Jane Randolph Jefferson, died at age 57.
May 7	Recovering from a severe migraine headache that had incapacitated him for five weeks, left Monticello to return to Congress and arrived in Philadelphia on May 14.
May 15	Congress resolved to form a government. Virginia Convention voted to instruct its delegates in Congress to propose independence, prepare a declaration of rights, and form a government.
May 27	Word of the Virginia Convention's resolutions of May 15 reached Philadelphia, and Jefferson began drafting a constitution for the state.
June 7	Richard Henry Lee introduced resolutions in Congress calling for independence, forming foreign alliances,

and preparing a plan for confederation of the colonies.

June 11   Congress appointed Jefferson, Franklin, John Adams,
               Robert R. Livingston, and Roger Sherman to prepare
               a declaration of independence.

June 20   Reappointed to serve another year in Congress.

June 28   Declaration of Independence presented to Congress.

June 29   Virginia Convention accepted the constitution prepared
               by George Mason with Jefferson's preamble, thus be-
               coming the first colony to form a government and be-
               come a state.

July 2   Congress approved Lee's resolution of June 7 calling
               for independence.

July 4   Congress accepted the Declaration of Independence.

September 2   Resigned from Congress because of his wife's ill
               health.

September 30   Appointed to negotiate trade and friendship treaties
               with France along with Silas Dean and Franklin. Re-
               fused on October 11 because of his wife's illness.

October 7   Took his seat in the Virginia House of Delegates and
               shortly thereafter introduced bills to establish a ju-
               diciary, revise the Virginia laws, and other basic
               measures.

November 5   Appointed to a committee along with George Wythe,
               Edmund Pendleton, George Mason, and Thomas L.
               Lee to revise Virginia's laws.

1777

January 13   The committee to revise Virginia's laws met in Fred-
               ricksburg. Mason and Lee dropped out because they
               were not lawyers.

May 20	Left the legislature until the fall session because of his wife's illness.
May 28	First (and only) son, unnamed, born. He died on June 14.
October 30	Attended the fall session of the Virginia Assembly.

1778
August 1	Fourth child, Mary ("Maria," "Polly"), born.

1779
February	Met with George Wythe and Edmund Pendleton to put their revision of the Virginia laws into final form.
June 1	Elected governor, succeeding Patrick Henry. Served until 1781 (two terms).

1780
During the year, he met a 22-year-old ex-soldier, James Monroe, who became a firm friend and follower.

November 3	Fifth child, Lucy Elizabeth, born.
December	Virginia Assembly voted to cede its claims to land northwest of the Ohio River to the United States.

1781
January 5	Benedict Arnold with 2,000 British troops captured Richmond, the new capital of Virginia.
April 15	Youngest daughter, Lucy Elizabeth, died at age of five months, reducing the family to two daughters, Martha and Maria.
June 2	Second term as governor expired. He had declined a third. The Assembly later in the month voted to investigate his governorship.

June 4	Barely escaped capture a second time when he left Monticello minutes before British cavalry arrived.
June	General Cornwallis occupied Elk Hill, one of Jefferson's plantations, and destroyed almost everything.
June 15	Named by Congress to the peace commission, joining John Adams, John Jay, Franklin, and Henry Laurens. He again declined because of his wife's health.
June 30	Fell from a horse, incapacitating himself for six weeks, during which time he began writing "Notes on Virginia."
October 19	Cornwallis surrendered at Yorktown.
November 30	Elected to Congress but declined because of his wife's health.
December 19	Answered the flimsy charges against him in the Assembly, and the Assembly unanimously voted his exoneration. He immediately left for Monticello, intending to retire from public life.

1782

May 6	Declined to take his seat in the Virginia House of Delegates because of his wife's health despite severe criticism from his friends who did not know the reasons.
May 8	Sixth child, named Lucy Elizabeth again, born.
September 6	His wife, Martha, never rallying from the birth of Lucy Elizabeth II four months earlier, died at age 33.
November 12	Appointed peace commissioner again. Accepted on November 26.
December 19	Left for Philadelphia to await a ship for England.

Waited there and in Baltimore for three and a half monghs.

1783

April 1   After news of the signing of the preliminary peace treaty with England on November 30, 1782, reached Congress, it decided there was no reason to send Jefferson to England.

April 19   Congress declared the end of the revolution--exactly eight years after the Battle of Lexington.

June   Drafted another constitution for Virginia in anticipation of a constitutional convention, but it was never called.

June 6   Elected to Congress for the 1783-84 session.

September 3   Peace treaty with England signed at Versailles.

November 14   Reached Annapolis, where Congress was meeting, but there was no quorum until December 13.

1784

January 14   Congress ratified the peace treaty, which had been referred to a committee Jefferson headed.

March 1   Virginia deeded the Northwest Territory to the nation.

March 12   Elected chairman of Congress, making him head of government despite his poor health.

April-May   Wrote instructions for ministers negotiating commercial treaties in Europe.

April   Wrote "Notes on the Establishment of a Money Unit and a Coinage for the United States," which proposed a decimal system (suggested by Gouverneur Morris) with a gold ten-dollar piece, a silver dollar, a silver tenth of a dollar, and a copper hundredth of a dollar.

April 23   Congress adopted Jefferson's "Report of Government for the Western Territory."

MINISTER ABROAD

May 7   Appointed a foreign minister to join Franklin and John Adams negotiating commercial treaties in Europe.

May 11   Left Annapolis to tour New England, taking his oldest daughter, Martha, with him.

June 26   Spain closed the Mississippi to American navigation.

July 5   Sailed from Boston and reached Paris on August 6.

1785

January 26   Received word of the death of his youngest daughter, Lucy II (2 1/2), from whooping cough on November 17, 1784.

March 10   Succeeded Franklin as Minister to France.

1786

January 16   The Virginia Assembly passed Jefferson's "Ordinance of Religious Freedom."

March 1   Reached London and tried, unsuccessfully, to help Adams negotiate trade treaties with England. Left for Paris on April 26.

1787

February 28   Left Paris on a tour of Southern France and Northern Italy. Returned early in June.

July 29   Youngest daughter, Maria, joined him and Martha in Paris.

October 12	Re-elected Minister to France for a three-year term.

1788

March 6	Left Paris to meet John Adams in The Hague before Adams returned to become Vice President. Then he toured some Northern German states and returned to Paris on April 23.

1789

April 30	Washington and Adams inaugurated in New York.
October 22	Left France on the <u>Claremont</u> for a leave in the United States.
November 23	Docked at Norfolk, Virginia, and soon learned he had been appointed Secretary of State on September 26. Reached Monticello in December.

1790

January 14	Alexander Hamilton, Secretary of the Treasury, submitted his first report on the public credit to the House of Representatives. (See excerpts in the <u>Washington</u> volume in this series.)
February 23	Oldest daughter, Martha, married Thomas Mann Randolph, Jr., her second cousin and son of Jefferson's old schoolmate, "Tuckahoe Tom" Randolph, at Monticello.

SECRETARY OF STATE

March 22	Sworn in as Secretary of State in New York.
July 16	Washington signed a bill establishing the seat of government in Philadelphia until 1800, when it would be permanently located near Georgetown on the Potomac--part of the bargain Jefferson made with Hamilton in return for passing Hamilton's assumption plan.

1791

February 15	Jefferson's opinion of the constitutionality of a national bank was opposed to the bill on the grounds of "strict construction."
February 23	Hamilton's opinion of the constitutionality of the national bank bill elaborated the doctrine of "implied powers." (See the Washington volume in this series for extracts of his opinion and of his report recommending a national bank.)
February 25	Washington signed a bill chartering a national bank.
March 14	Vermont became the first new state to join the Union.
May 17	Left Philadelphia, the new capital, with James Madison on a 920-mile trip through New York State, Vermont, and Connecticut, ostensibly for "scientific" purposes but really to line up political support. Returned on June 19.
October 31	First issue of the National Gazette, an anti-administration newspaper partly financed by the editor, Philip Freneau (a Princeton classmate of Madison's), through a State Department sinecure as a translator.
December 15	Bill of Rights adopted.

1792

February 20	Independent Post Office established, a blow to Jefferson, who wanted it placed under the State Department.
April	National Gazette began direct attacks on Hamilton and his party with Madison's blast, "Who are the real friends of the Union?"
July-December	Hamilton, in articles in John Fenno's Gazette of the United States signed "Catullus," attacked Jefferson, making him the leader of the anti-federalist party then taking shape.

August 26	Washington wrote Jefferson and Hamilton asking them to reconcile their differences.
September 9	Both replies to Washington's letters were that neither would retreat from his position. Jefferson said he intended to retire at the end of Washington's first term.
October 1	Washington tried to persuade Jefferson, visiting at Mount Vernon, not to retire.
October	During the month, news of the suspension of Louis XVI reached Philadelphia.
October 20	Washington placed the new U.S. Mint under Jefferson.
December	News of the creation of the French Republic reached Philadelphia.
December 5	Presidential electors case their ballots in their own states.
December 27	A resolution in the House of Representatives began an investigation of Hamilton's handling of the Treasury.

1793

January 3	Expressed his approval, in general, of the French Revolution in the "Adam and Eve" letter to William Short.
January 23	Watched the first balloon ascent in the United States from a prison yard in Philadelphia. Representative William Branch Giles of Virginia launched an attack on Hamilton and his policies with the first five Giles resolutions asking for more information. Congress accepted all of them.
February 7	Told Washington he would remain in office "perhaps till summer, perhaps till autumn."

February 8   Jean-Baptiste Ternant, the French Minister, urgently
                 requested immediate payment of $554,500 on the
                 U.S. debt to France. Jefferson approved of the ad-
                 vance payment, Hamilton disapproved. On February
                 25, Washington told Termant he could have the money.

February 27   Second set of Giles resolutions introduced in the
                 House. They were defeated on March 2.

March 4   Washington and Adams inaugurated for second time.

March 16   News of the execution of Louis XVI on January 21
                 arrived along with rumors of war in Europe.

April 7   Informed Washington of the French declaration of
                 war against England and Holland on February 1.

April 8   Edmond Charles Genet, the new French Minister,
                 landed at Charlestown, South Carolina, and began
                 commissioning privateers to attack British ships.

April 19   In a Cabinet meeting, Jefferson opposed issuing a
                 proclamation of neutrality and said that the 1778
                 treaty with France was still binding.

April 22   Washington issued the Proclamation of Neutrality
                 without using the word "neutrality."

May 2   Received the first of a series of complaints about
                 activities of American privateers outfitted by Genet.

May 15   Asked Ternant to release the British ship Grange,
                 which the French had captured in Delaware Bay and
                 brought into Philadelphia.

May 16   Genet arrived in Philadelphia to a tumultuous public
                 welcome.

May 22   Genet requested the United States to repay the entire
                 $2.5 million owed to France at once.

May 25   England and Spain signed an alliance.

May 27   Genet agreed to release the Grange, but insisted the
                  treaty of 1778 was still in effect and gave France the
                  right to bring prizes into American ports and do what
                  she wanted with them.

June 5   Genet agreed to stop commissioning privateers and
                  recruiting troops to attack British and Spanish ter-
                  ritories.

June 11   Sent Genet a letter agreeing to pay at once only 20%
                  of the loan due France during 1793.

June 14   Genet challenged the American refusal to permit him
                  to outfit privateers and threatened to appeal from the
                  President to "higher authority" (Congress and the
                  people).

June 17   Answered Genet's letters of June 14, and explained
                  the laws and government of the United States.

June 29   Gazette of the United States published the first of a se-
                  ries of articles by Hamilton (signed "Pacificus") push-
                  ing the executive department's power to the extreme.
                  The last article appeared on July 20.

July 7   Warned Genet not to send the Little Sarah, a British
                  ship captured by the French and brought into Phila-
                  delphia to be commissioned as a privateer and named
                  the Little Democrat, to sea. Genet sent the ship to
                  sea a few days later.

July 31   Told Washington he intended to resign as Secretary of
                  State at the end of September.
                  The first of Hamilton's "No Jacobin" letters appeared
                  in a New York newspaper and began running in the
                  Gazette of the United States August 31.

August 2	Washington, with the consent of his cabinet, decided to ask for Genet's recall.
August 11	Agreed to remain Secretary of State until the end of the year.
August–November	Yellow fever epidemic erupted in Philadelphia. All political activity halted with the exodus of government officials.
August 24	The first of Madison's "Helvidius" articles refuting Hamilton's "Pacificus" articles ran in the National Gazette. The last appeared on September 18.
August 28	Warned Governor Shelby of Kentucky to be alert for illegal efforts to recruit Americans to attack Spanish Louisiana.
September 15	Sent Genet a copy of the letter to France requesting his recall and a warning that he could continue to function as minister until his recall only so long as he obeyed our laws.
September 17	Left Philadelphia for Monticello and returned to Germantown, the temporary seat of the government, on November 1.
October 26	The last issue of the National Gazette was published. It had run into financial problems, and Freneau had resigned his post with the State Department. During the month, Hamilton and other Federalists raised money to keep Fenno's Gazette of the United States alive.
December 16	Gave Congress recommendations on foreign trade and a confidential report on unsettled negotiations with Spain.
December 31	Submitted his formal resignation to Washington. Ed-

mond Randolph became the new Secretary of State on
January 4.

IN THE WINGS

1794

January 5   Left Philadelphia for Monticello. Remained at home
                 until he returned to Philadelphia to become Vice Presi-
                 dent three years later.

April 25   Wrote John Adams that the only mistake he made in
                 retiring was not doing it four years earlier.

August-   Suffered an acute rheumatism attack which put him
September   in bed for two months. He believed this episode
                 marked the start of the decline in his health.

September 7   Received a letter from Secretary of State Edmond
                 Randolph asking him to become a special emissary
                 to negotiate a treaty with Spain on navigation on the
                 Mississippi, right of deposit at New Orleans, and
                 Indian affairs. He declined and Thomas Pinckney
                 was appointed.

November   Records showed he owned about 150 slaves--50 less
                 than a decade earlier. Most had been sold to repay
                 the Wayles' debts.

December 8   Wrote Madison, then in the House, of his doubts of
                 Washington's judgment in speaking against the demo-
                 cratic societies in his annual address on November
                 19--starting the split which widened between him and
                 Jefferson.

1795

January 31   Hamilton resigned as Secretary of the Treasury.

June 24   The Senate, meeting in special session, reluctantly
                 ratified the treaty Jay had signed with England on

	November 19, w ith one article referred back for re-negotiation.
July 14	Mobs in several cities protested Jay's treaty and, in Philadelphia, burned him in effigy.
July 21	Received a copy of the supposedly secret treaty, which had been printed in newspapers in June. He denounced it strongly in private in the months that followed but took no part in the public outcry. The treaty was his second major difference with Washington.
August 19	Edmond Randolph resigned as Secretary of State after Washington confronted him with an intercepted letter from Fauchet containing incriminating (but false) statements.
November 17	Washington appointed Secretary of War Timothy Pickering to be Secretary of State after five others had refused the post.
December 31	Wrote Giles that a firm party stand was needed.

1796

February 26	Madison wrote Monroe in France that he and other Republicans were goint to "push" Jefferson for President but feared he would refuse.
February 29	Washington proclaimed Jay's treaty in effect after Great Britain accepted the Senate's amendments.
March 3	The Senate approved the treaty Thomas Pinckney signed with Spain on October 27, 1795, giving the United States the right of deposit at New Orleans.
March 27	Wrote Madison he suspected Washington was being used as a front by the Federalists.

June 17   Wrote Washington he was not responsible for confidential information published in the Aurora. Washington replied on July 6, reiterating his faith in Jefferson but saying he had heard intimations of his disloyalty. It was the last exchange of letters between the two.

September 19   Washington's Farewell Address appeared in the Philadelphia Daily American Advertiser.

November 15   Pierre Adet, the French Minister, charged that Jay's treaty violated the 1778 treaty with France and suspended diplomatic relations.

November 21   Jefferson mortgaged 150 slaves to get funds to pay debts and remodel Monticello.

December 5   Presidential electors met in their respective states and cast their ballots.

December 17   Wrote Madison that, in event of a tie, he preferred the House elect Adams rather than him.

December 31   Received a letter from Madison saying he was probably elected Vice President.

1797

February 9   Formal counting of the electoral votes gave Adams 71 votes and the Presidency, Jefferson 68 and the Vice Presidency.

February 20   Left Monticello; arrived in Philadelphia March 2.

March 3   Adams asked Jefferson to undertake a mission to France, but he refused.

VICE PRESIDENT

March 4   Sworn in as Vice President; then Adams took the oath as President.

March 10	Presented a paper to the American Philosophical Society on the bones of a large animal he had found and called the "Megalonyx" or "great claw."
March 13	Left Philadelphia for Monticello after the Senate adjourned. Returned May 11.
May 9	While en route to Philadelphia, heard that his letter to Philip Mazzei of March 24, 1796, criticizing the Federalist Party, had been printed in garbled form in the newspapers.
May 16	Special session of Congress convened to hear Adams's report of the French refusal to receive C. C. Pinckney as minister the preceding December and Adams's request for defensive measures. Jefferson interpreted the speech as an indication Adams had joined the High Federalists and he turned away from his old friend and began to act as the leader of the opposition.
May 22	A federal grand jury in Richmond charged Samuel J. Cabell, congressman of the district encompassing Albemarle County, with slander of the federal government and attempting to increase foreign influence for statements in a circular letter to his constituents.
June 17	Wrote Aaron Burr, the most prominent Republican north of Philadelphia, to restore good relations despite his distrust of him. This was one of Jefferson's first actions as the leader of a political party.
June 20	Gave James Thomas Callender $15.14 in advance for copies of A History of the United States in 1796, then in preparation. Over the next year or so, Jefferson gave him about $200, ostensibly for books but often listed as charity in his accounts.
July 6	Left Philadelphia for Monticello and did not return until December.

July   Callender's History of the United States in 1796 ap-
                peared as a series of pamphlets and as a book on the
                19th.

August   Drew up a petition to the Virginia House of Delegates
                from voters in his congressional district protesting
                the infringment of legislators' freedom from coercion
                by the executive or judiciary shown in the Cabell case.

September 28   Callender, who had fled to Virginia from Philadelphia,
                wrote Jefferson asking for help. Jefferson sent him
                $50 through intermediaries.

October 13   His second living daughter, Maria, married John
                Wayles Eppes, her cousin, at Monticello.

December 12   Arrived in Philadelphia to preside over the Senate,
                which had convened November 13. The Senate was
                two-thirds Federalist; the House was about evenly
                divided.

                            1798
January 8   Adams announced the Eleventh Amendment (proposed
                on March 5, 1794) was ratified.

February 28   Joshua Coit of Connecticut read a garbled version of
                Jefferson's letter to Mazzei in the House and said,
                "Nothing but treason and insurrection would be the
                result of such opinions."

March 19   Adams told Congress that negotiations with France
                had failed and a state of quasi-war existed.

March 21   Wrote Madison that Adams's "war message" two days
                earlier was "insane" or at least "almost insane."

April 3   Adams released the XYZ Papers to Congress, as re-
                quested in Giles's resolution passed on April 2. A
                loud, angry cry arose from people in both parties.

April 15   Wrote Monroe that he thought the Federalists were opening his mail. His suspicions were correct.

April 26   Wrote Madison that Republican congressmen, unable to block Federalist war measures, were leaving Philadelphia in droves, leaving Swiss-born Albert Gallatin to lead the Republicans in the House.

April 30   Congress created the Navy Department.

May 4   A letter describing Jefferson's "moldboard of least resistance" (the cutting edge of a plow) was read to the American Philosophical Society.

May 21   Benjamin Stoddert named Secretary of the Navy.

June 13   Congress suspended trade with France and her colonies.

June 18   Congress passed the Naturalization Act, which extended the residence required for citizenship to 14 years. The period was restored to five years in 1802.

June 21   Adams told Congress he had recalled Gerry from France and would not send another minister until he was assured of a respectful reception.

June 22   Congress authorized Adams to appoint officers for an army of 10,000.

June 25   Congress passed the Alien Act, which gave the President the authority to expel dangerous aliens. Adams deported no one before the act expired in 1802.

June 26   Benjamin Franklin Bache, grandson of Benjamin Franklin and editor of the Aurora, the most influential Republican newspaper, was presented in federal court on common-law charges of seditious libel. The trial was set for October.

June 27	Left Philadelphia for Monticello, although Congress was still in session. Returned in mid-December.
July 6	Adams signed the Alien Enemies Act, which called for expulsion of citizens of belligerent nations in time of war--the only one of the Alien and Sedition Acts the Republicans supported.
July 7	Congress repealed the 1778 alliance with France.
July 14	Congress passed the Sedition Act, which called for imprisonment for conspiring against the government and for "false, scandalous, and malicious" speaking or writing about the government or its officials. It remained in force until March 3, 1801.
August	Meetings protesting the Sedition Act held in Virginia and other states during the month.
September 10	Benjamin Franklin Bache died of yellow fever before he could be brought to trial for seditious libel. William Duane took over as editor of the Aurora.
October 9	After an ultimatum from Washington, appointed to command the army on July 3, that he would resign unless Hamilton were made second in command rather than Knox or C. C. Pinckney, Adams gave Hamilton the post. Republican Matthew Lyon of Vermont convicted of seditious libel.
November 16	The Kentucky Resolutions, which Jefferson wrote secretly in September to protest the constitutionality of the Alien and Sedition Acts, were signed by the governor after passing the Kentucky House on November 10 and the Senate on the 13th. (Adams in this series contains the text of the Kentucky and Virginia Resolutions as well as the laws they were protesting.)

November 20   Undeclared naval war began with the French capture
                of the American schooner Retaliation off Guadeloupe.

November 29   Received a letter from the former French minister,
                Adet, then in France, saying that the Directorate
                wanted to remain at peace with the United States de-
                spite the efforts of "secret friends of Great Britain"
                in America.

December 21   Virginia Resolutions, written by Madison, passed the
                House of Delegates and the Senate three days later.
                They were more moderate than Jefferson's Kentucky
                Resolutions.
                Congressman Harrison Gray Otis wrote Hamilton ask-
                ing his advice. The military bills Otis introduced
                thereafter were Hamilton's, not Adams's.

                            1799
February 9   The Constitution captured the French frigate L'Insur-
                gante off Nevis--the new U.S. Navy's first battle test.

February 18   Without consulting Federalists in Congress, Adams
                nominated William Vans Murray, then Minister to
                The Hague, Minister to France after Murray wrote
                him that the French had said they would treat him with
                respect.

March 1   Left Philadelphia; reached Monticello March 8 and re-
                mained there until December.

March 12   Adams pardoned the leaders of the Fries Rebellion in
                eastern Pennsylvania the previous month against the
                advice of his cabinet and then left for Quincy, where
                he remained until October.

April 22   Wrote Edmond Pendleton that he believed Hamilton
                would be the real commander of the army, that the
                army would be used against dissenters (primarily Re-
                publicans), and that Hamilton would not disband the
                army, which Jefferson estimated at 44,000 men.

June 6	Patrick Henry died.
September 6	Paid Callender $50 in advance for copies of The Prospect Before Us, then in preparation, after seeing part of it.
October 16	Adams, after Secretary of State Pickering had neglected to send Chief Supreme Court Justice Oliver Ellsworth and North Carolina Governor William R. Davie to join Murray in France, despite Adams's instructions to do so in August, ordered them to depart. They left on November 3 but did not begin negotiations until spring, when the Directorate had been replaced by Napoleon's Consulate.
November 14	The Kentucky legislature passed Jefferson's second set of resolutions.
December 14	George Washington died at Mount Vernon.
December 21	Left Monticello; arrived in Philadelphia December 28, spending the national day of mourning for Washington (December 26) traveling.

1800

Census found the nation's population to be 5,300,000.

January 9	Wrote Thomas McKean, Republican Governor of Pennsylvania, supporting the request of John Beckley, former clerk of the House of Representatives, for an appointment--an action which indicated Jefferson's acceptance of the spoils system to a degree.
January 18	Wrote Dr. Joseph Priestly for advice on subjects to be taught in a university.
February 4	By this date, Jefferson had learned of the death of his daughter Maria's first child (a daughter) and of Jupiter, his coachman and traveling companion since his student days.

March 27   As presiding officer, signed a warrant for Duane's
                  arrest for contempt of the Senate for refusing to ap-
                  pear and defend himself on charges of defaming that
                  body. Duane eluded arrest while continuing to pub-
                  lish the Aurora.

April 12   Wrote DuPont de Nemours asking for his ideas on
                  higher education.

April 30   Thomas Cooper was convicted of seditious libel for
                  remarks about Adams in a pamphlet published the
                  preceding fall.

May   Federalist congressional caucuses nominated Adams
                  for a second term and C. C. Pinckney for Vice Presi-
                  dent.
                  Adams rid his cabinet of two of his secret enemies:
                  he accepted Secretary of War McHenry's resignation
                  on the 6th, the day after he accused him of not co-
                  operating; on the 12th he dismissed Secretary of State
                  Pickering, who had refused to resign.

May 10   Hamilton broke with Adams completely, saying he
                  would not support the President directly even if his
                  refusal meant Jefferson's election.

May 11   A Republican caucus adopted the first national plat-
                  form and, Jefferson's candidacy already settled, picked
                  Burr to run for Vice President.

May 14   The Senate asked Adams to prosecute Duane under
                  the Sedition Act. Adams took no action.

May 15   Left Philadelphia, arrived at Monticello on the 29th,
                  and stayed there until he departed for the new capital,
                  Washington, D.C., in November.

June 3   Callender convicted of seditious libel for statements
                  against Adams in The Prospect Before Us.

June 30   The Baltimore <u>American</u> printed a report, but said it might be false, on the death of Jefferson.

July 3   The <u>Aurora</u> said reports of Jefferson's death were false, but the false accounts spread faster than the truth for a time.

August 13   Wrote to Cotton Mather Smith, a New England clergyman, denying charges that he had acquired his property through fraud and deceit. Otherwise, he ignored charges of corruption, immorality, and atheism in the election campaign.

September 23   In a letter to Dr. Rush, wrote, "I have sworn upon the altar of God eternal hostility against every form of tyranny over the mind of man."

September 30   Convention of 1800 was signed in Paris (after Napoleon amended it), releasing the United States from the Treaty of 1778 and ending the quasi-war with France.

October 1   France regained Louisiana in a secret agreement with Spain (the Treaty of Ildefonso).

October 31   First issue of Samuel Harrison Smith's <u>National Intelligencer,</u> a Republican newspaper, appeared in Washington.

November 1   Adams became the first occupant of the still-unfinished "President's House."

November 17   The first session of Congress to meet in the new capital convened in the North Wing of the Capitol, the only finished part of the building.

November 24   Left Monticello for the new capital and arrived on the 27th.

December 3   Presidential electors cast their ballots.

December 12   The National Intelligencer reported that South Caro-
                  lina had chosen Republican electors, giving the Re-
                  publicans the Presidency.
                  Jefferson received a letter from South Carolina say-
                  ing that one of the state's electors would throw a
                  vote to George Clinton, giving Burr only seven elec-
                  toral votes and Jefferson eight and the presidency.

December 15   Wrote Burr to sound him out on his position in the
                  event of a tie in the electoral college, in which case
                  the Federalist House might refuse to choose a win-
                  ner and let the president pro tempore of the Senate,
                  a Federalist, act in lieu of a president.

December 16   By this date, Hamilton was saying Jefferson was pref-
                  erable to Burr because he was "at least honest"
                  whereas Burr was not to be trusted.

December 28   Learned that he and Burr were tied when the last
                  electoral returns were presented to him as the Sen-
                  ate's presiding officer.

December 31   National Intelligencer published extracts from a let-
                  ter Burr had written to General Samuel Smith of
                  Maryland on December 16 disclaiming any ambition
                  to be President in case of a tie vote. Later Burr
                  learned that there was indeed a tie and was angry
                  at the publication of the letter.

                                    1801
January 1   Received a letter from Burr, dated December 23,
                  pledging his support in the event of a tie and dis-
                  claiming any interest in the Presidency. Throughout
                  the next two months, however, Burr refused to re-
                  move himself from contention by a public statement
                  or even an unequivocal disavowal in private.

January 4	Wrote his daughter Maria that Federalist electors had offered Burr their votes for the Presidency, but that Burr had refused.
	General Samuel Smith visited Burr in Philadelphia and came away with the impression that Burr believed the House should elect him President if it could not elect Jefferson.
January 6	Monroe wrote Jefferson of the rumor that Congress would pick John Marshall or someone else to act as President until another election could be held.
January 9	Hamilton, answering a letter from Gouverneur Morris which told of a plan to let the president pro tempore of the Senate act as President, wrote that such a plan would be "dangerous and unbecoming."
January 10	The Aurora published a scheme, supposedly devised in the home of Justice Samuel Chase, to have the Chief Justice assume the Presidency if the House could not reach a decision.
January 15	By this date, Federalists in the House had decided to back Burr.
January 31	John Marshall, nominated on January 20 and approved by the Senate on January 27, sworn in as Chief Justice.
February 11	Presiding over a joint session of Congress, Jefferson opened the electoral votes and announced the results: 73 votes for himself and Burr, 65 for Adams, 64 for C. C. Pinckney, and one for John Jay. The House immediately went into session alone and began to vote, one vote for each of the 16 states.
February 13	Adams signed the Judiciary Act, which reduced the number of Justices from six to five and established 16 circuit courts--an attempt to retain Federalist control of the judiciary after losing the executive and both Houses of Congress.

February 16   The Gazette of the United States reported that the Republicans were ready to march on Washington if the House did not pick a President.

February 17   After 35 ballots in five days with the same result (8 states for Jefferson, 6 states for Burr, and 2 states with evenly divided delegations and therefore not voting), Federalists in the divided Maryland and Vermont delegations abstained, giving Jefferson 10 votes and the Presidency. The Delaware and South Carolina delegations, which had voted for Burr, abstained on the final (36th) ballot, giving him only 4 votes.

February 27   Samuel Harrison Smith published A Manual of Parliamentary Practice for the Use of the Senate of the United States, which Jefferson began writing shortly before becoming presiding officer in 1797. It is still part of the Senate manual and used in the House when no other rules apply.

March 3   Adams signed the last of his "midnight appointments," including 23 additional judges.

FIRST TERM

March 4   Sworn in as President by Chief Justice John Marshall --the first President inaugurated in the new capital.

March 5   Appointments of James Madison as Secretary of State, Henry Dearborn of Maine as Secretary of War (held over from Adams's administration), and Levi Lincoln of Massachusetts as Attorney General and ad interim Secretary of State all sent to the Senate and confirmed the same day.

April 1   Appointed General Samuel Smith ad interim Secretary of the Navy.

May 14	Albert Gallatin began serving as Secretary of the Treasury (recess appointment). Tripoli declared war on the United States. By this date, Jefferson had heard rumors that Spain had ceded Louisiana and East and West Florida to France.
May 20	Although unaware of Tripoli's declaration of war, sent four warships to the Mediterranean in response to the Pasha of Tripoli's demand the preceding fall for additional tribute.
July 27	Robert Smith began serving as Secretary of the Navy (recess appointment).
July 30	Left Washington to stay at Monticello, as he did every summer while in office to avoid the "sickly season." Returned to Washington September 30.
November 28	Appointed Gideon Granger of Connecticut Postmaster General and gave him Cabinet rank--the first head of the post office to be admitted to the inner circle.
December 7	First session of the Seventh Congress convened. It was overwhelmingly Republican; the Federalists were no longer significant opposition.
December 8	Sent his first annual message to Congress in writing instead of delivering it orally as Washington and Adams had done. (He was a poor public speaker and had, reportedly, a thin, high voice.)
December 17	Hamilton, writing as "Lucius Crassus," began publishing a series of articles bitterly attacking Jefferson's annual message in the New York Evening Post. The last one appeared on April 8, 1802.
December 19	Senate ratified the Convention of 1800 with France containing Napoleon's amendment of July 31.

1802

January 26   Senate confirmed Jefferson's recess appointments of Gallatin, Smith, and Granger.

February 6   Congress declared war on Tripoli.

March 8   Signed a bill repealing the Judiciary Act of 1801, abolishing Adams's circuit judges and restoring six justices as the number on the Supreme Court bench.

March 16   Army Engineer Corps established.
                  U.S. Military Academy authorized. Opened at West Point July 4, 1802.

April 6   A bill abolishing all internal taxes passed.

April 18   Wrote Robert R. Livingston, minister to France, to try to get Napoleon to cede New Orleans and the Floridas to the United States.

April 29   Congress passed a new Judiciary Act establishing six federal judicial circuits.

May 2   U.S. Patent Office organized; Dr. William Thornton appointed "supervisor."

July   Callender's attacks on Jefferson began.

August 23   By this date, Jefferson knew Morocco had declared war on the United States.

October 18   The Spanish Intendent at New Orleans withdrew the United States' right of deposit. Jefferson learned of it late in November.

October 30   Thomas Paine arrived in Philadelphia on a merchant ship after refusing Jefferson's offer of passage on a Navy vessel returning from France. Jefferson invited him to stay at the White House and later at Monticello despite objections of political allies and enemies.

November 3   Explained his Indian policy to Chief Handsome Lake.

December 15   Sent his second annual message to Congress, which
              had convened on December 6.

                              1803

January 11   Nominated James Monroe to be minister extraordi-
              nary with wide discretionary powers to join Living-
              ston in negotiating with France to purchase Louisiana.

January 18   In a confidential message to the House, proposed
              sending an expedition to explore Louisiana, follow
              the Missouri River to its source, and go on to the
              Pacific.

February 18   Ohio became the 17th state.

February 24   The Supreme Court, in Marbury v. Madison, de-
              clared a portion of the Judiciary Act of 1789 uncon-
              stitutional--the first ruling on the constitutionality
              of a law.

February 26   Congress appropriated $2 million for expenses in
              negotiations with France.

April 11   Livingston wrote Jefferson that Talleyrand had of-
              fered to sell the whole of Louisiana and that he had
              first said no but then said he would reconsider and
              talk the offer over with Monroe when he arrived.

April 12   Monroe arrived in Paris to join the negotiations with
              the French finance minister, Barbe-Marbois, who
              had been put in charge of the negotiations when Na-
              poleon heard that the United States had appropriated
              $2 million "to bribe the French negotiators."

April 14   Marbois offered to sell all of Louisiana for 100 mil-
              lion francs (about $18 million). The next day, Mon-
              roe and Livingston offered half that amount.

April 30   Monroe and Livingston agreed to buy Louisiana for
                    60 million francs to be paid to France and 20 million
                    to be paid to Americans to repay French debts (about
                    $15 million in all).

May 17   Right of deposit at New Orleans restored.

July 3   Learned of Louisiana Purchase.

October 17   Congress met early to approve the Louisiana Purchase
                    Treaty. Jefferson's third annual message announced
                    the purchase and the fact that no new taxes were needed
                    to pay for it. Both Jefferson's sons-in-law (Thomas
                    Mann Randolph, Jr., and John Wayles Eppes) were
                    new members of the House.

October 20   The Senate approved the Louisiana Purchase Treaty.

October 25   The House approved a financial bill needed to put the
                    Louisiana Purchase Treaty into effect, and the Senate
                    passed it the next day. Jefferson signed it October 30.

November 30   Spain formally ceded her claims to Louisiana to the
                    French in accordance with the treaty signed October
                    1, 1800.

December 12   The Twelfth Amendment, calling for separate votes
                    for President and Vice President, proposed to the
                    states.

December 20   United States took formal possession of Louisiana.

                                    1804
February 25   Republican congressional caucus unanimously nomi-
                    nated Jefferson for a second term. George Clinton,
                    Governor of New York for 18 years, nominated for
                    Vice President.

March 12   The Senate removed Thomas Pickering, a federal

district judge in New Hampshire from office--the first impeachment of a federal judge. He was clearly insane.
The House voted to attempt to impeach Justice Chase.

March 26   Appointed William Johnson of South Carolina to the Supreme Court.

April 1   Left Washington for Monticello; returned May 13.

April 17   Maria, Mrs. John Wayles Eppes, died at Monticello, leaving Martha sole survivor of the six children Jefferson had.

May 14   Lewis and Clark left St. Louis on their way to the Pacific.

June 3   In reply to a letter from Abigail Adams expressing her condolences at the death of Maria, he tried to heal the breach between her husband and himself. However, she took offense at Jefferson's criticism of Adams's "midnight appointments," and the estrangement continued.

July 11   Burr shot Hamilton in a duel. Hamilton died the next day and Burr fled to South Carolina to escape prosecution for murder while continuing as Vice President until his term expired.

November   States chose presidential and vice-presidential electors. Jefferson and Clinton received 162 votes to C. C. Pinckney and Rufus King's 14.

November 8   Fourth annual message to Congress.

December 31   Attorney General Levi Lincoln resigned.

1805

January 29   Debate of the Yazoo claims began in the House and lasted until February 2.

March 1   The Senate acquitted Justice Chase in an impeach-
                 ment attempt.

                          SECOND TERM

March 4   Inaugurated for his second term. Held over all cabi-
                 net members from his first term.

June 4   Peact treaty with Tripoli signed. A few days later
                 another was signed with Morocco, ending the Barbary
                 states' interference with U.S. shipping.

August 7   Appointed John Breckinridge of Kentucky Attorney
                 General (recess appointment).

November 7   Lewis and Clark sighted the Pacific and reached it
                 eight days later.

December 3   Sent his fifth annual message to Congress.

December 6   Sent Congress a secret message on the dispute with
                 Spain over the boundaries of Louisiana.

                              1806
January 11   The House authorized $2 million for the purchase of
                 East and West Florida from Spain.

January 17   Sent a special message to Congress on British cap-
                 tures of American ships and impressment of Ameri-
                 can seamen.
                 Martha Jefferson Randolph gave birth to James Madi-
                 son Randolph, Jefferson's grandson and the first
                 child born in the White House.

March 29   Congress authorized construction of the Cumberland
                 Road to Ohio.

April 15   Bill prohibiting importation of articles from or made
                 in England after November 15, 1806, passed the

Senate. It had been accepted by the House March 26.

May 16 — British Orders in Council declared the coasts of France and Germany under blockade.

September-
October — Heard vague rumors of a plot by Burr in the West. In October, Jefferson warned the governors of the Mississippi and Orleans Territories and military commanders to be on the alert and also sent a special agent with wide civil and military powers to investigate and act if necessary.

October 20 — Learned that Lewis and Clark had returned to St. Louis on September 23.

November 3 — The U.S. Attorney in Kentucky attempted to have the district court in Frankfort bring Burr before it to answer charges of unlawful activity. The judge refused but ordered a grand jury to investigate. When the District Attorney was unable to bring key witnesses before two successive grand juries, the judge dismissed the charges.

November 10 — Appointed Henry Brockholst Livingston of New York to the Supreme Court.

November 13 — Lieutenant Zebulon Pike discovered the Colorado mountain later named after him.

November 21 — Napoleon declared the British Isles under blockade ("Berlin Decree").

November 25 — Received a message from General James Wilkinson, commander of the army in Louisiana, informing him of Burr's plot.
Wilkinson reached New Orleans, proclaimed martial law, and began organizing a defense.

November 27 — Issued a proclamation warning people to withdraw from illegal activities and ordered the army and militia to seize people and equipment connected with Burr's plot.

December 2	Sent his sixth annual message to Congress.
December 6	Congress passed and Jefferson signed a bill delaying execution of the non-importation act until July 1, 1807, and giving him the authority to suspend enforcement until December, 1807, at his discretion.
December 14	Attorney General Breckinridge died.

1807

January 7	George III issued his second set of Orders in Council prohibiting trade with France. During the month, Burr surrendered in the Mississippi Territory and appeared before the Territorial Court, which discharged him for lack of evidence. Wilkinson sent soldiers to arrest him, and he fled.
January 20	Appointed Caesar Augustus Rodney of Delaware Attorney General.
January 22	Sent the House, as requested, an outline of what he knew of the Burr conspiracy and the civil and·military measures it took to suppress it.
February	Burr, traveling in Alabama in disguise, was captured.
March 3	Allowed the Ninth Congress to expire without presenting to the Senate the treaty Monroe and William Pinkney had signed with England on December 31 because it did not end British impressment of American sailors. Appointed Thomas Todd of Kentucky to the Supreme Court.
March 26	Preliminary hearing of charges against Burr began in Richmond, Virginia, presided over by Chief Justice Marshall and the district judge.

January 20   Appointed Caesar Augustus Rodney of Delaware Attorney General.

January 22   Sent the House, as requested, an outline of what he knew of the Burr conspiracy and the civil and military measures it took to suppress it.

February   Burr, traveling in Alabama in disguise, was captured.

March 3   Allowed the Ninth Congress to expire without presenting to the Senate the treaty Monroe and William Pinkney had signed with England on December 31 because it did not end British impressment of American sailors.
                Appointed Thomas Todd of Kentucky to the Supreme Court.

March 26   Preliminary hearing of charges against Burr began in Richmond, Virginia, presided over by Chief Justice Marshall and the district judge.

May 22	Grand jury hearing on Burr's conspiracy began.
June 22	British ship Leopard fired on the American Chesapeake, boarded her, and seized American seamen.
June 24	Burr indicted for treason and a misdemeanor (waging war against Spain).
July 2	Banned British ships from American waters. A British squadron, however, remained just off the coast.
August 3	Burr's trial for treason started.
August 7	Robert Fulton's steamboat cruised on the Hudson River.
August 31	Burr acquitted of treason.
October 20	Burr acquitted of the misdemeanor, and Marshall committed him for trial in Ohio on a misdemeanor, under $3,000 bond. Burr jumped bail and fled to Europe.
October 26	Congress convened early in anticipation of a reply from England to demands for reparations for damage to the Chesapeake. Jefferson's seventh annual message presented the next day.
November 11	George III issued a third set of Orders in Council barring trade with France.
November 23	Sent Congress, as requested, a detailed account of the procedings and testimony in the Burr trial.
December 17	Napoleon forbade trade with England and subjected violators' ships to confiscation ("Milan Decree").
December 18	Sent Congress a confidential message containing the

British and French proclamations concerning treatment of neutral ships and asked for an embargo to
prevent American ships from engaging in foreign commerce. The Senate passed the Embargo Act the same
day.

December 22   The House passed the Embargo Act and Jefferson
signed it. In the next few months, Congress passed
a number of bills increasing the strength of the army,
the navy, and harbor fortifications and authorizing the
states to raise and equip larger militias.

1808

January 1   A law prohibiting importation of slaves, passed March
2, 1807, became effective.

January 23   Republican congressional caucus met and nominated
Madison to run for President and Clinton for Vice
President again.

March 17   British envoy sent to negotiate the Chesapeake episode
broke off the talks before they got started and returned
to England.

March 18   Wrote Monroe to reaffirm his friendship and also to
convince Monroe not to run for President with the back-
ing of dissident Republicans ("Quids") and the few
Federalists still in Congress. Monroe accepted Jefferson on both counts.

April 9   Vote to expel John Smith of Ohio from the Senate for
taking part in Burr's conspiracy fell one vote short of
the two-thirds majority needed.

August 15   Advised the governor of New York to call out part of
the militia to halt smuggling on the Canadian border.
Military force became necessary to enforce the embargo in several New England ports.

September 23   British Minister of Foreign Affairs George Canning
                firmly rejected William Pinkney's overtures for set-
                tling the <u>Chesapeake</u> episode and other issues.

November   Madison elected President with 122 electoral votes to
                C. C. Pinckney's 47; Clinton elected Vice President
                with 113 votes to Rufus King's 47.

November 8   Sent his eighth and last message to Congress.

November 22   The House resolved that the embargo continue. The
                Senate approved a similar resolution December 2.

December 21   The Senate passed a bill containing measures for en-
                forcing the embargo. The law stirred up a storm in
                New England, and some town meetings voted for "dis-
                union."

                                1809
February 17   Appointed John Smith <u>ad interim</u> Secretary of War.

March 3   Signed a bill repealing the Embargo Act and another
                (Non-Importation Act) prohibiting trade with England
                and France.

                            RETIREMENT

March 4   Attended the inauguration of Madison and Clinton.

March 11   Left Washington for the last time.

                                1812
January   Resumed correspondence with John Adams through
                the mediation of Dr. Benjamin Rush, long a corre-
                spondent of both.

June 18   Congress declared war on Great Britain.

Fall   Refused several overtures to run for President and a

suggestion from Madison that he become Secretary
of State.

November
Madison re-elected President; Elbridge Gerry elected
Vice President.

1814
August 25
Wrote a letter to Edward Coles expressing his long-
standing views of slavery.

November
Declined to serve another term as president of the
American Philosophical Society, a post he had held
since 1797.

September 21
Offered to sell his library (some 10,000 volumes) to
Congress as the nucleus of a new collection to replace
the one destroyed when the British burned Washington
the preceding summer.

1815
February 11
News of the signing of the Treaty of Ghent ending the
war on December 24, 1814, reached Washington and
Monticello two days later.

1816
November
James Monroe elected President; Daniel Tompkins
elected Vice President.

1817
May
Met with Madison, Monroe, and other members of
the "Board of Visitors" to begin planning Central College in Charlottesville, which became the University
of Virginia.

1819
During the year, cosigned a $20,000 note for Wilson
Cary Nicholas.

January
A bill creating the University of Virginia passed by
the Virginia Assembly.

February   Jefferson appointed one of the members of the Board
                    of Visitors for the new university.

March 29   Appointed Rector (President) of the new university.
                    During the next few years, he spent a great deal of
                    time designing buildings and supervising their con-
                    struction.

                              1820
November   Monroe re-elected President and Tompkins Vice Pres-
                    ident.

                              1823
October 24   Wrote Monroe giving his views on the involvement of
                    European nations in the American hemisphere. Mon-
                    roe incorporated many of Jefferson's ideas in the Mon-
                    roe Doctrine, which he proclaimed on December 2.

                              1824
November   Lafayette, on a triumphal tour of the nation, visited
                    Monticello.
                    John Q. Adams elected President; John C. Calhoun Vice
                    President.

                              1825
April 1   The University of Virginia opened.

Summer   Lafayette again visited Jefferson before returning to
                    France.

                              1826
January 20   Requested the Virginia Assembly to pass a special bill
                    permitting him to sell his property by lottery to raise
                    money to pay his debts--over $100,000, including the
                    note he signed for Wilson Cary Nicholas, who had gone
                    bankrupt.

February 7   Refused an interest-free loan of $80,000 from the Vir-
                    ginia Assembly in lieu of permission to sell his prop-
                    erty by lottery.

February 20　　The Virginia Assembly gave Jefferson permission to hold a lottery. Contributions flooded in at first, but soon dwindled to a trickle, and the lottery was never held.

March 16　　　Wrote his will. Gave gifts to John Adams and his own grandchildren and freedom to five of his slaves.

June 26　　　Wrote his last letter to the Mayor of Washington, declining because of his health to attend the celebration of the fiftieth anniversary of the signing of the Declaration of Independence on July 4 with the other surviving signers.

July 4　　　　Died at Monticello, age 83, a few hours before John Adams died in Braintree, Massachusetts. He was buried at Monticello beside his wife and daughter in a private funeral the next day.

DOCUMENTS

SUMMARY VIEW OF THE RIGHTS OF BRITISH AMERICA
August, 1774

Anticipating attending the First Virginia Convention, which was to convene on August 1, Jefferson wrote a long, detailed essay listing the colonies' grievances against the British. He could not attend because of illness, but he sent a copy to Payton Randolph, his cousin, who placed it before the Convention. The meeting adopted a more moderate statement, but Jefferson's essay was printed in Williamsburg before the month was over and later in England by Edmond Burke and others sympathetic to the colonies. "Summary" contained almost every idea to be found in the Declaration of Independence, written two years later. This excerpt is the peroration.

. . . . That these are our grievances, which we have thus laid before his Majesty, with that freedom of language and sentiment which becomes a free people, claiming their rights as derived from the laws of nature, and not as the gift of their chief magistrate. Let those flatter, who fear: it is not an American art. To give praise where it is not due might be well from the venal, but would ill beseem those who are asserting the rights of human nature. They know, and will, therefore, say, that Kings are the servants, not the proprietors of the people. Open your breast, Sire, to liberal and expanded thought. Let not the name of George the Third be a blot on the page of history. You are surrounded by British counsellors, but remember that they are parties. You have no ministers for American affairs, because you have none taken from among us, nor amenable to the laws on which they are to give you advice. It behoves you, therefore, to think and to act for yourself and your people. The great principles of right and wrong are legible to every reader; to pursue them, requires not the aid of many counsellors. The whole art of government consists in the art of being honest. Only aim to do your duty, and mankind will give you credit where you fail. No longer persevere in sacrificing the rights of one part of the empire to the inordinate desires of another; but deal out to all equal and impartial right. Let no act be passed by any one legislature which may infringe on the rights and liberties of another. This is the important post in which fortune has placed you, holding the balance of a great, if a well-poised empire. This, Sire, is the advice of your great American council, on the observance of which may perhaps depend your felicity and future fame, and the preservation of that harmony which alone can continue, both to Great Britain and America, the reciprocal advantages of their connection. It is neither our wish nor our interest

to separate from her. We are willing, on our part, to sacrifice everything which reason can ask, to the restoration of that tranquility for
which all must wish. On their part, let them be ready to establish
union on a generous plan. Let them name their terms, but let them be
just. Accept of every commercial preference it is in our power to give,
for such things as we can raise for their use, or they make for ours.
But let them not think to exclude us from going to other markets, to
dispose of those commodities which they cannot use, nor to supply
those wants which they cannot supply. Still less, let it be proposed,
that our properties, within our own territories, shall be taxed or regu-
lated by any other power on earth but our own. The God who gave us
life, gave us liberty, at the same time: the hand of force may destroy,
but cannot disjoin them. This Sire, is our last, our determined resolution. And that you will be pleased to interpose, with that efficacy which
your earnest edeavors may insure, to procure redress of these our
great grievances, to quiet the minds of your subjects in British America, against any apprehensions of future encroachment, to establish
fraternal love and harmony through the whole empire, and that that
may continue to the latest ages of time, is the fervent prayer of all
British America.

DECLARATION OF INDEPENDENCE
July 4, 1776

The other members of the committee elected to prepare a declaration of Independence prevailed upon Jefferson to draft it, and he wrote it within a few days without consulting anyone or any written sources. The committee made a few minor changes and then submitted the document to Congress. Congress made more extensive changes, primarily to avoid alienating English friends of the colonies. This is the copy finally approved by Congress.

A Declaration by the Representatives of the United States of America, in General Congress assembled.

When, in the course of human events, it becomes necessary for one people to dissolve the political bands which have connected them with another, and to assume among the powers of the earth the separate and equal station to which the laws of nature and of nature's God entitle them, a decent respect to the opinions of mankind requires that they should declare the causes which impel them to the separation.

We hold these truths to be self-evident: that all men are created equal; that they are endowed by their creator with certain inalienable rights; that among these are life, libert, and the pursuit of happiness; that to secure these rights, governments are instituted among men, deriving their just powers from the consent of the governed; that whenever any form of government becomes destructive of these ends, it is the right of the people to alter or to abolish it, and to institute new government, laying its foundation on such principles, and organizing its powers in such form, as to them shall seem most likely to effect their safety and happiness. Prudence, indeed, will dictate that governments long established should not be changed for light and transient causes; and accordingly all experience hath shown that mankind are more disposed to suffer while evils are sufferable, than to right themselves by abolishing the forms to which they are accustomed. But when a long train of abuses and usurpations pursuing invariably the same object, evinces a design to reduce them under absolute despotism, it is their right, it is their duty to throw off such government, and to provide new guards for their future security. Such has been the patient sufferance of these Colonies; and such is now the necessity which constrains them to alter their former systems of government. The history of the present King of Great Britain is a history of repeated injuries and usurpations, all having in direct object the establishment of an absolute tyranny over these States. To prove this, let facts be submitted to a candid world.

He has refused his assent to laws the most wholesome and necessary for the public good.

He has forbidden his governors to pass laws of immediate and pressing importance, unless suspended in their operation till his assent should be obtained; and, when so suspended, he has utterly neglected to attend to them.

He has refused to pass other laws for the accommodation of large districts of people, unless those people would relinquish the right of representation in the Legislature, a right inestimable to them, and formidable to tyrants only.

He has called together legislative bodies at places unusual, uncomfortable, and distant from the depository of their public records, for the sole purpose of fatiguing them into compliance with his measures.

He has dissolved representative houses repeatedly for opposing with manly firmness his invasions on the rights of the people.

He has refused for a long time after such dissolutions to cause others to be elected, whereby the legislative powers, incapable of annihilation, have returned to the people at large for their exercise, the State remaining, in the meantime, exposed to all the dangers of invasion from without and convulsions within.

He has endeavored to prevent the population of these States; for that purpose obstructing the laws for naturalization of foreigners, refusing to pass others to encourage their migrations hither, and raising the conditions of new appropriations of lands.

He has obstructed the administration of justibe by refusing his assent to laws for establishing judiciary powers.

He has made judges dependent on his will alone for the tenure of their offices, and the amount and payment of their salaries.

He has erected a multitude of new offices, and sent hither swarms of new officers to harass our people and eat out their substance.

He has kept among us in times of peace standing armies without the consent of our Legislatures.

He has affected to render the military independent of, and superior to, the civil power.

He has combined with others to subject us to a jurisdiction foreign to our constitutions and unacknowledged by our laws, giving his assent to their acts of pretended legislation for quartering large bodies of armed troops among us; for protecting them by a mock trial from punishment for any murders which they should commit on the inhabitants of these States; for cutting off our trade with all parts of the world; for imposing taxes on us without our consent; for depriving us in many cases of the benefits of trial by jury; for transporting us beyond seas to be tried for pretended offences; for abolishing the free system of English laws in a neighboring province, establishing therein ar arbitrary government, and enlarging its boundaries, so as to render it at once an example and fit instrument for introducing the same absolute rule into these Colonies; for taking away our charters, abolishing our most valuable laws, and altering fundamentally the forms of our governments; for suspending our own Legislatures, and declaring themselves invested with power to legislate for us in all cases whatsoever.

He has abdicated government here by declaring us out of his protection, and waging war against us.

He has plundered our seas, ravaged our coasts, burnt our towns, and destroyed the lives of our people.

He is at this time transporting large armies of foreign mercenaries to complete the works of death, desolation, and tyranny already begun with circumstances of cruelty and perfidy scarcely paralleled in the most barbarous ages, and totally unworthy the head of a civilized nation.

He has constrained our fellow-citizens taken captive on the high seas to bear arms against their country, to become the exectutioners of their friends and brethren, or to fall themselves by their hands.

He has excited domestic insurrection among us, and has endeavored to bring on the inhabitants of our frontiers the merciless Indian savages, whose known rule of warfare is an undistinguished destruction of all ages, sexes, and conditions.

In every stage of these oppressions we have petitioned for redress in the most humble terms: our repeated petitions have been answered only by repeated injuries.

A Prince whose character is thus marked by every act which may define a tyrant is unfit to be the ruler of a free people.

Nor have we been wanting in attentions to our British brethren. We have warned them from time to time of attempts by their legislature to extend an unwarantable jurisdiction over us. We have reminded them of the circumstances of our emigration and settlement here, we have appealed to their native justice and magnanimity and we have conjured them by the ties of our common kindred to disavow these usurpations which would inevitably interrupt our connections and correspondence. They too have been deaf to the voice of justice and of consanguinity. We must therefore acquiesce in the necessity which denounces our separation and hold them as we hold the rest of mankind, enemies in war, in peace friends.

We therefore the representatives of the United States of America in General Congress assembled, appealing to the supreme judge of the world for the rectitude of our intentions, do in the name, and by the authority of the good people of these Colonies, solemnly publish and declare, that these united Colonies are, and of right ought to be, free and independent States; that they are absolved from all allegiance to the British crown, and that all political connection between them and the state of Great Britain is, and ought to be, totally dissolved; and that as free and independent States, they have full power to levy war, conclude peace, contract alliances, establish commerce, and to do all other acts and things which independent States may of right do.

And for the support of this declaration, with a firm reliance on the protection of divine providence, we mutually pledge to each other our lives, our fortunes, and our sacred honor.

NOTES ON VIRGINIA
1784

*During July, 1781, Jefferson began organizing the notes he
had been taking for years on the flora, fauna, geography,
geology, meteorology, Indians, Negroes, slavery, religion,
farming, manufacturing, government, and other aspects of
Virginia and, to a lesser extent, the rest of the nation, into a comprehensive, coherent description. He had 200
copies of the document, his only full-length book, published soon after he reached France in 1784, and sent copies
to scholars in Europe and America. Other versions, authorized and not, soon appeared.* Notes *gave Jefferson a
shining reputation as a scientist and scholar. Later,
political opponents misinterpreted parts of it to attack
him. Opponents twisted this section to "prove" that he
was an atheist.*

. . . The error seems not sufficiently eradicated, that the operations of the mind, as well as the acts of the body, are subject to the
coercion of the laws. But our rulers can have no authority over such
natural rights, only as we have submitted to them. The rights of conscience we never submitted, we could not submit. We are answerable
for them to our God. The legitimate powers of government extend to
such acts only as are injurious to others. But it does me no injury for
my neighbor to say there are twenty gods, or no God. It neither picks
my pocket nor breaks my leg. If it be said his testimony in a court of
justice cannot be relied on, reject it then, and be the stigma on him.
Constraint may make him worse by making him a hypocrite, but it
will make him a truer man. It may fix him obstinately in his errors,
but will not cure them. Reason and free inquiry are the only effectual
agents against error. Give a loose to them, they will support the true
religion, by bringing every false one to their tribunal, to the test of
their investigation. They are the natural enemies of error, and of
error only. . . .

REPORT OF GOVERNMENT FOR THE
WESTERN TERRITORIES
April 23, 1784

Jefferson's report recommended forming new states of the
land northwest of the Ohio River rather than, as some
wished, making colonies of it. Congress adopted the plan
but deleted a portion which barred slavery from the new
territories after 1800, and also dropped Jefferson's names
and boundaries, Congress later incorporated the principle
of creating new states in the Northwest Ordinance of 1787.

The Committee to whom was recommitted the report of a plan for
a temporary government of the western territory have agreed to the
following resolutions.

Resolved, that so much of the territory ceded or to be ceded by
individual states to the United States as is already purchased or shall
be purchased of the Indian inhabitants and offered for sale by Congress,
shall be divided into distinct states, in the following manner, as nearly
as such cessions will admit; that is to say, by parallels of latitude,
so that each state shall comprehend from north to south two degrees
of latitutde beginning to count from the completion of forty-five degrees north of the equator; and by meridians of longitude, one of which
shall pass thro' the lowest point of the rapids of Ohio, and the other
through the Western Cape of the mouth of the Great Kanhaway,. . .

That the settlers on any territory so purchased, and offered for
sale, shall, either on their own petition, or on the order of Congress,
receive authority from them with appointments of time and place for
their free males of full age, within the limits of their state to meet
together for the purpose of establishing a temporary government, to
adopt the constitution and laws of any one of the original states, so
that such laws nevertheless shall be subject to alteration by their ordinary legislature, and to erect, subject to a like alteration, counties
or townships for the election of members for their legislature.

That when any such State shall have acquired twenty thousand inhabitants, on giving due proof thereof to Congress, they shall receive
from them authority with appointment of time and place to call a convention of representatives to establish a permanent Constitution and
Government for themselves. Provided that both the temporary and permanent governments be established on these principles as their basis.

First. That they shall forever remain a part of this confederacy of
the United States of America. Second. That they shall be subject to the
articles of Confederation in all those cases in which the original states
shall be so subject and to all the acts and ordinances of the United
States in Congress assembled, conformable thereto. Third. That they
shall in no case interfere with the primary disposal of the soil by the

United States . . . nor with the ordinances and regulations which Congress may find necessary for securing the title to such soil to the bona fide purchasers. Fourth. That they shall be subject to pay a part of the federal debts contracted or to be contracted, to be apportioned on them by Congress, according to the same common rule and measure, by which apportionments thereof shall be made on the other states. Fifth. That no tax shall be imposed on lands, the property of the United States. Sixth. That their respective governments shall be republican. Seventh. That the lands of non-resident proprietors shall in no case, be taxed higher than those of residents... before the admission thereof to a vote by its delegates in Congress.

That whensoever any of the said states shall have, of free inhabitants, as many as shall then be in any one the least numerous of the thirteen Original states, such State shall be admitted by its delegates into the Congress of the United States on an equal footing with the said original states: provided the consent of so many states in Congress is first obtained as may at the time be competent to such admission. And in order to adopt the said Articles of Confederation to the state of Congress when it's numbers shall be thus increased, it shall be proposed to the legislatures of the states originally parties thereto, to require the assent of two thirds of the United States in Congress assembled in all those cases wherein by the said articles the assent of nine states is now required; which being agreed to by them shall be binding on the new states. Unitl such admission by their delegates into Congress, any of the said states after the establishment of their temporary government shall have authority to keep a sitting member in Congress, with a right of debating, but not of voting. . . .

That the preceding articles shall be formed into a charter of compact, shall be duly executed by the President of the United States in Congress assembled, under his hand and the seal of the United States, shall be promulgated and shall stand as fundamental constitutions between the thirteen original states and each of the several states now newly described, unalterable but by the joint consent of the United States in Congress assembled, and of the particular state within which such alteration is proposed to be made.

VIRGINIA STATUTE FOR RELIGIOUS FREEDOM
January 16, 1786

*Jefferson included a bill establishing complete religious
freedom in his revision of the Virginia laws, and almost
every year thereafter, he or his friends introduced virtual-
ly the same bill, only to have it rejected. When he was in
France, Madison, Wilson Cary Nicholas and other friends
sponsored it again, and it passed. It became the model for
the First Ammendment to the Constitution, and Jefferson
ranked it in importance along with the Declaration of Independence and the founding of the University of Virginia.
Below is Jefferson's draft of the bill as modified by the
Virginia Legislature.*

Well aware that Almighty God hath created the mind free; that all
attempts to influence it by temporal punishments or burdens, or by
civil incapacitations, tend only to beget habits of hypocrisy and mean-
ness, and are a departure from the plan of the Holy Author of our
religion, who being Lord both of body and mind, yet chose not to prop-
agate it by coercions on either, as was in his Almighty power to do;
that the impious presumption of legislators and rulers, civil as well
as ecclesiastical, who, being themselves but fallible and uninspired
men, have assumed dominion over the faith of others, setting up
their own opinions and modes of thinking as the only true and infal-
liable, and as such endeavoring to impose them on others, hath established and maintained false religions over the greatest part of the
world, and through all time: that to compel a man to furnish contributions of money for the propagation of opinions which he disbelieves
is sinful and tyrannical, that even the forcing him to support this or
that teacher of his own religious persuasion, is depriving him of the
comfortable liberty of giving his contributions to the particular pastor
whose morals he would make his pattern, and whose powers he feels
most persuasive to righteousness, and is withdrawing from the ministry those temporal rewards, which proceeding from an approbation
of their personal conduct, are an additional incitement to earnest and
unremitting labors for the instruction of mankind; that our civil rights
have no dependence on our religious opinions, any more than our
opinions in physics or geometry; that, therefore, the proscribing any
citizen as unworthy the public confidence by laying upon him as in-
capacity of being called to the offices of trust and emolument, unless
he profess or renounce this or that religious opinion, is depriving
him injuriously of those privileges and advantages to which, in common with his fellow-citizens, he has a natural right; that it tends also
to corrupt the principles of that very religion it is meant to encourage,
by bribing, with a monopoly of worldly honors and emoluments, those
who will externally profess and conform to it; that though indeed these
are criminal who do not withstand such temptation, yet neither are

those innocent who lay the bait in their way; that to suffer the civil magistrate to intrude his powers into the field of opinion and to restrain the profession or propagation of principles, on the supposition of their ill tendency is a dangerous fallacy, which at once destroys all religious liberty, because he being of course judge of that tendency will make his opinions the rule of judgment, and approve or condemn the sentiments of others only as they shall square with or differ from his own; that it is time enough for the rightful purposes of civil government for its officers to interfere when principles break out into overt acts against peace and good order; and finally, that truth is great and will prevail if left to herself; that she is the proper and sufficient antagonist to error, and has nothing to fear from the conflict unless by human interposition disarmed of her natural weapons, free argument and debate; errors ceasing to be dangerous when it is permitted freely to contradict them.

Be it therefore enacted by the General Assembly, That no man shall be compelled to frequent or support any religious worship, place, or ministry whatsoever, nor shall be enforced, restrained, molested, or burthened in his body or goods, nor shall otherwise suffer, on account of his religious opinions or belief; but that all men shall be free to profess, and by argument to maintain, their opinions in matters of religion, and that the same shall in no wise diminish, enlarge, or affect their civil capacities.

And though we know well that this Assembly, elected by the people for the ordinary purposes of legislation only, have no power to restrain the acts of succeeding Assemblies, constituted with the power equal to our own, and that therefore to declare this act irrevocable would be of no effect in law; yet we are free to declare, and do declare, that the rights hereby asserted are of the natural rights of mankind, and that if any act shall be hereafter passed to repeal the present or to narrow its operation, such act will be an infringement of natural right.

JEFFERSON'S OPINION OF THE CONSTITUTIONALITY
OF THE NATIONAL BANK BILL
February 15, 1791

*When Washington asked for opinions on the constitutional-
ity of the National Bank Bill, Edmond Randolph, the
Attorney General, said it was not. Jefferson said it was
unconstitutional on "strict constructionist" grounds.
Hamilton argued at length that the bill was legal on the
basis of "implied powers," despite the Tenth Ammendment which was to be in force before the year was out.
See Hamilton's main points in the Washington volume in
this series.*

The bill for establishing a National Bank undertakes among other
things: —

1. To form the subscribers into a corporation.

2. To enable them in their corporate capacities to receive grants
of land; and so far is against the laws of Mortmain.

3. To make alien subscribers capable of holding lands; and so far
is against the laws of alienage.

4. To transmit these lands, on the death of a proprietor; to a certain
line of successors; and so far changes the course of Descents.

5. To put the lands out of the reach of forfeiture or escheat; and
so far is against the laws of Forfeiture and Escheat.

6. To transmit personal chattels to successors in a certain line;
and so far is against the laws of Distribution.

7. To give them the sole and exclusive right of banking under the
national authority; and so far is against the laws of Monopoly.

8. To communicate to them a power to make laws paramount to
the laws of the States; for so they must be construed, to protect the
institution from the control of the State legislatures; and so, probably,
they will be construed.

I consider the foundation of the Constitution as laid on this ground:
That "all powers not delegated to the United States, by the Constitution, nor prohibited by it to the States, are reserved to the States or
to the people." (XIIth amendment.)* To take a single step beyond the
boundaries thus specially drawn around the powers of Congress, is
to take possession of a boundless field of power, no longer susceptible of any definition.

---

* Ed. Note: Actually the present 10th amendment, two proposed amendments never
having been ratified.

The incorporation of a bank, and the power assumed by this bill, have not, in my opinion, been delegated to the United States, by the Constitution.

I. They are not among the powers specially enumerated: for these are:

1st. A power to lay taxes for the purpose of paying the debts of the United States; but no debt is paid by this bill, nor any tax laid. Were it a bill to raise money, its orgination in the Senate would condemn it by the Constituion.

2d. "To borrow money." But this bill neither borrows money nor ensures the borrowing it. The proprietors of the bank will be just as free as any other money holders, to lend their money to the public. The operation proposed in the bill, first, to lend them two millions, and then to borrow them back again, cannot change the nature of the latter act, which will still be a payment, and not a loan, call it by what name you please.

3. To "regulate commerce with foreign nations, and among the States, and with the Indian tribes." To erect a bank, and to regulate commerce, are very different acts. He who erects a bank, creates a subject of commerce in its bills; so does he who makes a bushel of wheat, or digs a dollar out of the mines; yet neither of these persons regulates commerce thereby. To make a thing which may be bought and sold, is not to prescribe regulations for buying and selling. Besides, if this was an exercise of the power of regulating commerce, it would be void, as extending as much to the internal commerce of every State, as to its external. For the power given to Congress by the Constitution does not extend to the internal regulation of the commerce of a State, (that is to say of the commerce between citizen and citizen), which remain exclusively with its own legislature; but to its external commerce only, that is to say, its commerce with another State, or with foreign nations, or with the Indian tribes. Accordingly the bill does not propose the measure as a regulation of trade, but as "productive of considerable advantages to trade." Still less are these powers covered by any other of the special enumerations.

II. Nor are they within either of the general phrases which are the two following: —

1. To lay taxes to provide for the general welfare of the United States, that is to say, "to lay taxes for the purpose of providing for the general welfare." For the laying of taxes is the power, and the general welfare the purpose for which the power is to be exercised. They are not to lay taxes ad libitum for any purpose they please; but only to pay the debts or provide for the welfare of the Union. In like manner, they are not to do anything they please to provide for the gen-

eral welfare, but only to lay taxes for that purpose. To consider the latter phrase, not as describing the purpose of the first, but as giving a distinct and independent power to do any act they please, which might be for the good of the Union, would render all the preceding and sub-sequent enumerations of power completely useless.

It would reduce the whole instrument to a single phrase, that of instituting a Congress with power to do whatever would be for the good of the United States; and, as they would be the sole judges of the good or evil, it would be also a power to do whatever evil they please.

It is an established rule of construction where a phrase will bear either of two meanings, to give it that which will allow some meaning to the other parts of the instrument, and not that which would render all the others useless. Certainly no such universal power was meant to be given them. It was intended to lace them up straitly within the enumerated powers, and those without which, as means, these powers could not be carried into effect. It is known that the very power now proposed as a means was rejected as and end by the Convention which formed the Constitution. A proposition was made to authorize Congress to open canals, and an amendatory one to empower them to incorporate. But the whole was rejected, and one of the reasons for rejection urged in debate was, that then they would have a power to erect a bank, which would render the great cities, where there were prejudices and jealousies on the subject, adverse to the reception of the Constitution.

2. The second general phrase is, "to make all laws necessary and proper for carrying into execution the enumerated powers." But they can all be carried into execution without a bank. A bank therefore is not necessary, and consequently not authorized by this phrase.

It has been urged that a bank will give great facility or convenience in the collection of taxes. Suppose this were true; yet the Constitution allows them only the means which are "necessary," not those which are merely "convenient" for effecting the enumerated powers. If such a latitude of construction be allowed to this phrase as to give any non-enumerated power, it will go to every one, for there is not one which ingenuity may not torture into a convenience in some instance or other, to some one of so long a list of enumerated powers. It would swallow up all the delegated powers, and reduce the whole to one power as before observed. There it was that the Constitution restrained them to the necessary means, that is to say, to those means without which the grant of power would be nugatory.

But let us examine this convenience and see what it is. The report on this subject, page 3, states the only general convenience to be, the preventing the transportation and re-transportation of money be-tween the States and the treasury, (for I pass over the increase of circulating medium, ascribed to it as a want, and which, according to my ideas of paper money, is clearly a demerit.) Every State will have to pay a sum of tax money into the treasury; and the treasury will have to pay, in every State, a part of the interest on the public debt, and salaries to the officers of government resident in that State. In most of the States there will still be a surplus of tax money to come up to the seat of government for the officers residing there. The payments of interest and salary in each State may be made by treasury orders on the State collector. This will take up the great export of the money he has collected in his State, and consequently prevent the great mass of it from being drawn out of the State. If there be a balance of commerce in favor of that State against the one in which the government resides, the surplus of taxes will be remitted by the bills of exchange drawn for that commercial balance. And so it must be if there was a bank. But if there be no balance of commerce, either direct or circuitous, all the banks in the world could not bring up the surplus of taxes, but in the form of money. Treasury orders then, and bills of exchange may prevent the displacement of the main mass of the money collected, without the aid of any bank, and where these fail, it cannot be prevented even with that aid.

Perhaps, indeed, bank bills may be a more convenient vehicle than treasury orders. But a little difference in the degree of convenience, cannot constitute the necessity which the constitution makes the ground for assuming any non-enumerated power.

Besides; the existing banks will, without a doubt, enter into arrangements for lending their agency, and the more favorable, as there will be a competition among them for it; whereas the bill delivers us up bound to the national bank, who are free to refuse all arrangement, but on their own terms, and the public not free, on such refusal, to employ any other bank. That of Philadelphia. I believe, now does this business, by their postnotes, which, by an arrangement with the treasury, are paid by any State collector to whom they are presented. This expedient alone suffices to prevent the existence of that necessity which may justify the assumption of an enumerated one. The thing may be done, and has been done, and well done, without this assumption, therefore, it does not stand on that degree of necessity which can honestly justify it.

It may be said that a bank whose bills would have a currency all over the States, would be more convenient than one whose currency is limited to a single State. So it would be still more convenient that there should be a bank, whose bills should have a currency all over the world. But it does not follow from this superior conveniency, that there exists anywhere a power to establish such a bank; or that the world may not go on very well without it.

Can it be thought that the Constitution intended that for a shade or two of convenience, more or less, Congress should be authorized to break down the most ancient and fundamental laws of the several States; such as those against Mortmain, the laws of Alienage, the rules of descent, the acts of distribution, the laws of escheat and forfeiture, the laws of monopoly? Nothing but a necessity invincible by any other means, can justify such a prostitution of laws, which constitute the pillars of our whole system of jurisprudence. Will Congress be too straight-laced to carry the constitution into honest effect, unless they may pass over the foundation-laws of the State government for the slightest convenience of theirs?

The negative of the President is the shield provided by the constitution to protect against the invasions of the legislature: 1. The right of the Executive, 2. Of the Judiciary. 3. Of the States and State legislatures. The present is the case of a right remaining exclusively with the States, and consequently one of those intended by the Constitution to be placed under its protection.

It must be added, however, that unless the President's mind on a view of everything which is urged for and against this bill, is tolerably clear that it is unauthorized by the Constitution; it the pro and the con hang so even as to balance his judgment, a just respect for the wisdom of the legislature would naturally decide the balance in favor of their opinion. It is chiefly for cases where they are clearly misled by error, ambition, or interest, that the Constitution has placed a check in the negative of the President.

FIRST INAUGURAL ADDRESS
March 4, 1801

Jefferson's inaugural address, coming after one of the most bitter, sordid campaigns on record, sought to reunite the nation — and also to draw Federalists, many of whom were appalled by their leaders' threats of anarchy, into Republican ranks. In the years that followed, he succeeded and the "Revolution of 1800", as Jefferson liked to call it, was bloodless.

Friends and Fellow-Citizens.

Called upon to undertake the duties of the first executive office of our country, I avail myself of the presence of that portion of my fellow-citizens which is here assembled to express my grateful thanks for the favor with which they have been pleased to look toward me, to declare a sincere consciousness that the task is above my talents, and that I approach it with those anxious and awful presentiments which the greatness of the charge and the weakness of my powers so justly inspire. A rising nation, spread over a wide and fruitful land, traversing all the seas with the rich productions of their industry, engaged in commerce with nations who feel power and forget right, advancing rapidly to destinies beyond the reach of mortal eye — when I contemplate these transcendent objects, and see the honor, the happiness, and the hopes of this beloved country committed to the issue and the auspices of this day, I shrink from the contemplation, and humble myself before the magnitude of the undertaking. Utterly, indeed, should I despair did not the presence of many whom I here see remind me that in the other high authorities provided by our Constitution I shall find resources of wisdom, of virtue, and of zeal on which to rely under all difficulties. To you, then, gentlemen, who are charged with the sovereign functions of legislation, and to those associated with you, I look with encouragement for that guidance and support which may enable us to steer with safety the vessel in which we are all embarked amidst the conflicting elements of a troubled world.

During the contest of opinion through which we have passed the animation of discussions and of exertions has sometimes worn an aspect which might impose on strangers unused to think freely and to speak and to write what they think; but this being now decided by the voice of the nation, announced according to the rules of the Constitution, all will, of course, arrange themselves under the will of the law, and unite in common efforts for the common good. All, too, will bear in mind this sacred principle, that though the will of the majority is in all cases to prevail, that will to be rightful must be reasonable; that the minority possess their equal rights, which equal law must protect, and to violate would be oppression. Let us, then, fellow-citizens, unite with one heart

and one mind. Let us restore to social intercourse that harmony and
affection without which liberty and even life itself are but dreary things.
And let us reflect that, having banished from our land that religious
intolerance under which mankind so long bled and suffered, we have
yet gained little if we countenance a political intolerance as despotic,
as wicked, and capable of as bitter and bloody persecutions. During the
throes and convulsions of the ancient world, during the agonizing
spasms of infuriated man, seeking through blood and slaughter his
long-lost liberty, it was not wonderful that the agitation of the billows
should reach even this distant and peaceful shore; that this should be
more felt and feared by some and less by others, and should divide
opinions as to measures of safety. But every difference of opinion is
not a difference of principle. We have called by different names brethren of the same principle. We are all Republicans, we are all Federalists. If there be any among us who would wish to dissolve this Union
or to change its republican form, let them stand undisturbed as monu-
ments of the safety with which error of opinion may be tolerated where
reason is left free to combat it. I know, indeed, that some honest men
fear that a republican government can not be strong, that this Government is not strong enough; but would the honest patriot, in the full
tide of successful experiment, abandon a government which has so far
kept us free and firm on the theoretic and visionary fear that this
Government, the world's best hope, may by possibility want energy to
preserve itself? I trust not. I believe this, on the contrary, the strong-
est Government on earth. I believe it the only one where every man,
at the call of the law, would fly to the standard of the law, and would
meet invasions of the public order as his own personal concern. Sometimes it is said that man can not be trusted with the government of
himself. Can he, then, be trusted with the government of others? Or
have we found angels in the forms of kings to govern him? Let history
answer this question.

Let us then, with courage and confidence pursue our own Federal
and Republican principles, our attachment to union and representative
government. Kindly separated by nature and a wide ocean from the
exterminating havoc of one quarter of the globe; too high-minded to
endure the degradations of the others; possessing a chosen country, with
room enough for our descendants to the thousandth and thousandth
generation; entertaining a due sense of our equal right to the use of our
own faculties, to the acquisitions of our own industry, to honor and
confidence from our fellow-citizens, resulting not from birth, but from
our actions and their sense of them; enlightened by a benign religion,
professed, indeed, and practiced in various forms, yet all of them in-
culcating honesty, truth, temperance, gratitude, and the love of man;
acknowledging and adoring an overruling Providence, which by all its
dispensations proves that it delights in the happiness of man here and
his greater happiness hereafter — with all these blessings, what more
is necessary to make us a happy and a prosperous people? Still one

thing more, fellow-citizens — a wise and frugal Government, which shall restrain men from injuring one another, shall leave them otherwise free to regulate their own pursuits of industry and improvement, and shall not take from the mouth of labor the bread it has earned. This is the sum of good government, and this is necessary to close the circle of our felicities.

About to enter, fellow-citizens, on the exercise of duties which comprehend everything dear and valuable to you, it is proper you should understand what I deem the essential principles of our Government, and consequently those which ought to shape its Administration. I will compress them within the narrowest compass they will bear, stating the general principle, but not all its limitations. Equal and exact justice to all men, of whatever state or persuasion, religious or political; peace, commerce, and honest friendship with all nations, entangling alliances with none; the support of the State governments in all their rights, as the most competent administrations for our domestic concerns and the surest bulwarks against antirepublican tendencies; the preservation of the General Government in its whole constitutional vigor, as the sheet anchor of our peace at home and safety abroad; a jealous care of the right of election by the people — a mild and safe corrective of abuses which are lopped by the sword of revolution where peaceable remedies are unprovided; absolute acquiescence in the decisions of the majority, the vital principle of republics, from which is no appeal but to force, the vital principle and immediate parent of despotism; a well-disciplined militia, our best reliance in peace and for the first moments of war, till regulars may relieve them; the supremacy of the civil over the military authority; economy in the public expense, that labor may be lightly burthened; the honest payment of our debts and sacred preservation of the public faith; encouragement of agriculture, and of commerce as its handmaid; the diffusion of information and arraignment of all abuses at the bar of the public reason; freedom of religion; freedom of the press, and freedom of person under the protection of the habeas corpus, and trial by juries impartially selected. These principles form the bright constellation which has gone before us and guided our steps through an age of revolution and reformation. The wisdom of our sages and blood of our heroes have been devoted to their attainment. They should be the creed of our political faith, the text of civic instruction, the touchstone by which to try the services of those we trust; and should we wander from them in moments of error or of alarm, let us hasten to retrace our steps and to regain the road which alone leads to peace, liberty, and safety.

I repair, then, fellow-citizens, to the post you have assigned me. With experience enough in subordinate offices to have seen the difficulties of this the greatest of all, I have learnet to expect that it will rarely fall to the lot of imperfect man to retire from this station with the reputation and the favor which bring him into it. Without pretensions to that high confidence you reposed in our first and greatest revolutionary character, whose preeminent services had entitled him to the first place in his country's love and destined for him the fairest page in the volume of faithful history, I ask so much confidence only as may give firmness and effect to the legal administration of your affairs. I shall often go wrong through defect of judgment. When right, I shall often be though wrong by those whose positions will not command a view of the whole ground. I ask your indulgence for my own errors, which will never be intentional, and your support against the errors of others, who may condemn what they would not if seen in all its parts. The approbation implied by your suffrage is a great consolation to me for the past, and my future solicitude will be to retain the good opinion of those who have bestowed it in advance, to conciliate that of others by doing them all the good in my power, and to be instrumental to the happiness and freedom of all.

Relying, then, on the patronage of your good will, I advance with obedience to the work, ready to retire from it whenever you become sensible how much better choice it is in your power to make. And may that Infinte Power which rules the destinies of the universe lead our councils to what is best, and give them a favorable issue for your peace and prosperity.

FIRST ANNUAL MESSAGE
December 8, 1801

Jefferson presented his first annual message in writing rather than orally as Washington and Adams had done. Subsequent presidents followed his example until Wilson was elected more than one hundred years later. Jefferson reported a world at peace, except for the Barbary States, and suggested general measures rather than specific recommendations, a policy he was to observe in all his annual messages.

Fellow-Citizens of the Senate and House of Representatives:

It is a circumstance of sincere gratification to me that on meeting the great council of our nation I am able to announce to them on grounds of reasonable certainty that the wars and troubles which have for so many years afflicted our sister nations have at length come to an end, and that the communications of peace and commerce are once more opening among them. Whilst we devoutly return thanks to the beneficent Being who has been pleased to breathe into them the spirit of conciliation and forgiveness, we are bound with peculiar gratitude to be thankful to Him that our own peace has been preserved through so perilous a season, and ourselves permitted quietly to cultivate the earth and to practice and improve those arts which tend to increase our comforts. The assurances, indeed, of friendly disposition received from all the powers with whom we have principal relations had inspired a confidence that our peace with them would not have been disturbed. But a cessation of irregularities which had affected the commerce of neutral nations and of the irritations and injuries produced by them can not but add to this confidence, and strengthens at the same time the hope that wrongs committed on unoffending friends under a pressure of circumstances will now be reviewed with candor, and will be considered as founding just claims of retribution for the past and new assurance for the future.

Among our Indian neighbors also a spirit of peace and friendship generally prevails, and I am happy to inform you that the continued efforts to introduce among them the implements and the practice of husbandry and of the household arts have not been without success; that they are becoming more and more sensible of the superiority of this dependence for clothing and subsistence over the precarious resources of hunting and fishing, and already we are able to announce that instead of that constant diminution of their numbers produced by their wars and their wants, some of them begin to experience an increase of population.

To this state of general peace with which we have been blessed, one only exception exists. Tripoli, the least considerable of the Barbary

States, had come forward with demands unfounded either in right or in compact, and had permitted itself to denounce war on our failure to comply before a given day. The style of the demand admitted but one answer. I sent a small squadron of frigates into the Mediterranean, with assurances to that power of our sincere desire to remain in peace, but with orders to protect our commerce against the threatened attack. The measure was seasonable and salutary. The Bey had already declared war. His cruisers were out. Two had arrived at Gibraltar. Our commerce in the Mediterranean was blockaded and that of the Atlantic in peril. The arrival of our squadron dispelled the danger. One of the Tripolitan cruisers having fallen in with and engaged the small schooner Enterprise, commanded by Lieutenant Sterret, which had gone as a tender to our larger vessels, was captured, after a heavy slaughter of her men, without the loss of a single one on our part. The bravery exhibited by our citizens on that element will, I trust, be a testimony to the world that it is not the want of that virtue which makes us seek their peace, but a conscientious desire to direct the energies of our nation to the multiplication of the human race, and not to its destruction. Unauthorized by the Constitution, without the sanction of Congress, to go beyond the line of defense, the vessel, being disabled from committing further hostilities, was liberated with its crew. The Legislature will doubtless consider whether, by authorizing measures of offense also, they will place our force on an equal footing with that of its adversaries. I communicate all material information on this subject, that in the exercise of this important function confided by the Constitution to the Legislature exclusively their judgment may form itself on a knowledge and consideration of every circumstance of weight.

I wish I could say that our situation with all the other Barbary States was entirely satisfactory. Discovering that some delays had taken place in the performance of certain articles stipulated by us, I thought it my duty, by immediate measures for fulfilling them, to vindicate to ourselves the right of considering the effect of departure from stipulation on their side. From the papers which will be laid before you you will be enabled to judge whether our treaties are regarded by them as fixing at all the measure of their demands or as guarding from the exercise of force our vessels within their power, and to consider how far it will be safe and expedient to leave our affairs with them in their present posture.

I lay before you the result of the census lately taken of our inhabitants, to a conformity with which we are now to reduce the ensuing ratio of representation and taxation. You will perceive that the increase of numbers during the last ten years, proceeding in geometrical ratio, promises a duplication in little more than twenty-two years. We contemplate this rapid growth and the prospect it holds up to us, not with a view to the injuries it may enable us to do others in some future day, but to the settlement of the extensive country still remaining vacant within our limits to the multiplication of men susceptible of happiness, educated in the love of order, habituated to self-government, and valuing its blessings above all price.

Other circumstances, combined with the increase of numbers, have produced an augmentation of revenue arising from consumption in a ratio far beyond that of population alone; and though the changes in foreign relations now taking place so desirably for the whole world may for a season affect this branch of revenue, yet weighing all probabilities of expense as well as of income, there is reasonable ground of confidence that we may now safely dispense with all the internal taxes, comprehending excise, stamps, auctions, licenses, carriages, and refined sugars, to which the postage on newspapers may be added to facilitate the progress of information, and that the remaining sources of revenue will be sufficient to provide for the support of Government, to pay the interest of the public debts, and to discharge the principals within shorter periods than the laws or the general expectation had contemplated. War, indeed, and untoward events may change this prospect of things and call for expenses which the imposts could not meet; but sound principles will not justify our taxing the industry of our fellow-citizens to accumulate treasure for wars to happen we know not when, and which might not, perhaps, happen but from the temptations offered by that treasure.

These views, however, of reducing our burthens are formed on the expectation that a sensible and at the same time a salutary reduction may take place in our habitual expenditures. For this purpose those of the civil Government, the Army, and Navy will need revisal.

When we consider that this Government is charged with the external and mutual relations only of these States; that the States themselves have principal care of our persons, our property, and our reputation, constituting the great field of human concerns, we may well doubt whether our organization is not too complicated, too expensive; whether offices and officers have not been multiplied unnecessarily and sometimes injuriously to the service they were meant to promote. I will cause to be laid before you an essay toward a statement of those who, under public employment of various kinds, draw money from the Treasury or from our citizens. Time has not permitted a perfect enumeration, the ramifications of office being too multiplied and remote to be completely traced in a first trial. Among those who are dependent on Executive disrection I have begun the reduction of what was deemed unnecessary. The expenses of diplomatic agency have been considerably diminished. The inspectors of internal revenue who were found to obstruct the accountability of the institution have been discontinued. Several agencies created by Executive authority, on salaries fixed by that also, have been suppressed, and should suggest the expediency of regulating that power by law, so as to subject its exercises to legislative isnepction and sanction. Other reformations of the same kind will be pursued with that caution which is requisite in removing useless things, not to injure what is retained. But the great mass of public offices is established by law, and therefore by law alone can be abolished. Should the Legislature think it expedient to pass this roll in review and try all its parts by the test of public utility, they may be assured of every aid and light which Executive information can yield. Considering the general tendency to multiply offices and dependencies and to increase expense to the ultimate term of burthen which the citizen can bear, it behooves us to avail ourselves of every occasion which presents itself for taking off the surcharge, that it never may be seen here that after leaving to labor the smallest portion of its earnings on which it can subsist, Government shall itself consume the whole residue of what it was instituted to guard.

In our care, too, of the public contributions intrusted to our direction it would be prudent to multiply barriers against their dissipation by appropriating specific sums to every specific purpose susceptible of definition; by disallowing all applications of money varying from the appropriation in object or transcending it in amount; by reducing the undefined field of contingencies and thereby circumscribing discretionary powers over money, and by bringing back to a single department all accountabilities for money, where the examinations may be prompt, efficacious, and uniform.

An account of the receipts and expenditures of the last year, as prepared by the Secretary of the Treasury, will, as usual, be laid before you. The success which has attended the late sales of the public lands shews that with attention they may be made an important source of receipt. Among the payments those made in discharge of the principal and interest of the national debt will shew that the public faith has been exactly maintained. To these will be added an estimate of appropriations necessary for the ensuing year. This last will, of course, be affected by such modifications of the system of expense as you shall think proper to adopt.

A statement has been formed by the Secretary of War, on mature consideration, of all the posts and stations where garrisons will be expedient and of the number of men requisite for each garrison. The whole amount is condiserably short of the present military establishment. For the surplus no particular use can be pointed out. For defense against invasion their number is as nothing, nor is it conceived needful or safe that a standing army should be kept up in time of peace for that purpose. Uncertain as we must ever be of the particular point in our circumference where an enemy may choose to invade us, the only force which can be ready at every point and competent to oppose them is the body of neighboring citizens as formed into a militia. On these, collected from the parts most convenient in numbers proportioned to the invading force, it is best to rely not only to meet the first attack, but if it threatens to be permanent to maintain the defense until regulars may be engaged to relieve them. These considerations render it important that we should at every session continue to amend the defects which from time to time shew themselves in the laws for regulating the mailitia until they are sufficiently perfect. Nor should we now or at any time separate until we can say we have done everything for the militia which we could do were an enemy at our door.

The provision of military stores on hand will be laid before you, that you may judge of the additions still requisite.

With respect to the extent to which our naval preparations should be carried some difference of opinion may be expected to appear, but just attention to the circumstances of every part of the Union will doubtless reconcile all. A small force will probably continue to be wanted for actual service in the Mediterranean. Whatever annual sum beyond that you may think proper to appropriate to naval preparations would perhaps be better employed in providing those articles which may be kept without waste or consumption, and be in readiness when any exigence calls them into use. Progress has been made, as will appear by papers now communicated, in providing materials for 74-gun ships as directed by law.

How far the authroity given by the Legislature for procuring and establishing sites for naval purposes has been perfectly understood and pursued in the execution admits of some doubt. A statement of the expenses already incurred on that subject is now laid before you. I have in certain cases suspended or slackened these expenditures, that the Legislature might determine whether so many yards are necessary as have been contemplated. The works at this place are among those permitted to go on, and five of the seven frigates directed to be laid up have been brought and laid up here, where, besides the safety of their position, they are under the eye of the Executive Administration, as well as of its agents, and where yourselves also will be guided by your own view in the legislative provisions respecting them which may from time to time be necessary. They are preserved in such condition, as well the vessels as whatever belongs to them, as to be at all times ready for sea on a short warning. Two others are yet to be laid up so soon as they shall have received the repairs requisite to put them also into sound condition. As a superintending officer will be necessary at each yard, his duties and emoluments, hitherto fixed by the Executive, will be a more proper subject for legislation. A communication will also be made of our progress in the execution of the law respecting the vessels directed to be sold.

The fortifications of our harbors, more or less advanced, present considerations of great difficulty. While some of them are on a scale sufficiently proportioned to the advantages of their position, to the efficacy of their protection, and the importance of the points within it, others are so extensive, will cost so much in their first erection, so much in their maintenance, and require such a force to garrison them as to make it questionable what is best now to be done. A statement of those commenced or projected, of the expenses already incurred, and estimates of their future cost, as far as can be foreseen, shall be laid before you, that you may be enabled to judge whether any alteration is necessary in the laws respecting this subject.

Agriculture, manufactures, commerce, and navigation, the four pillars of our prosperity, are then most thriving when left most free to individual enterprise. Protection from casual embarrassments, however, may sometimes be seasonably interposed. If in the course of your observations or inquiries they should appear to need any aid within the limits of our constitutional powers, your sense of their importance is a sufficient assurance they will occupy your attention. We can not, indeed, but all feel an anxious solicitude for the difficulties under which our carrying trade will soon be placed. How far it can be relieved, otherwise than by time, is a subject of important consideration.

The judiciary system of the United States, and especially that portion of it recently erected, will of course present itself to the contemplation of Congress, and, that they may be able to judge of the proportion which the institution bears to the business it has to perform, I have caused to be procured from the several States and now lay before Congress an exact statement of all the causes decided since the first establishment of the courts, and of those which were depending when additional courts and judges were brought in to their aid.

And while on the judiciary organization it will be worthy your consideration whether the protection of the inestimable institution of juries has been extended to all the cases involving the security of our persons and property. Their impartial selection also being essential to their value, we ought further to consider whether that is sufficiently secured in those States where they are named by a marshal depending on Executive will or designated by the court or by officers dependent on them.

I can not omit recommending a revisal of the laws on the subject of naturalization. Considering the ordinary chances of human life, a denial of citizenship under a residence of fourteen years is a denial to a great proportion of those who ask it, and controls a policy pursued from their first settlement by many of these States, and still believed of consequence to their prosperity; and shall we refuse to the unhappy fugitives from distress that hospitality which the savages of the wilderness extended to our fathers arriving in this land? Shall oppressed humanity find no asylum on this globe? The Constitution indeed has wisely provided that for admission to certain offices of important trust a residence shall be required sufficient to develop character and design. But might not the general character and capabilities of a citizen be safely communicated to everyone manifesting a bona fide purpose of embarking his life and fortunes permanently with us, with restrictions, perhaps, to guard against the fraudulent asurpation of our flag, an abuse which brings so much embarrassment and loss on the genuine citizen and so much danger to the nation of being involved in war that no endeavor should be spared to detect and suppress it?

These, fellow-citizens, are the matters respecting the state of the nation which I have thought of importance to be submitted to your consideration at this time. Some others of less moment or not yet ready for communication will be the subject of separate messages. I am happy in this opportunity of committing the arduous affairs of our Government to the collected wisdom of the Union. Nothing shall be wanting on my part to inform as far as in my power the legislative judgment, nor to carry that judgment into faithful execution. The prudence and temperance of your discussions will promote within your own walls that conciliation which so much befriends rational conclusion, and by its example will encourage among our constituents that progress of opinion which is tending to unite them in object and in will. That all should be satisfied with any one order of things is not to be expected; but I indulge the pleasing persuasion that the great body of our citizens will cordially concur in honest and disinterested efforts which have for their object to preserve the General and State Governments in their constitutional form and equilibrium; to maintain peace abroad, and order and obedience to the laws at home; to establish principles and practices of administration favorable to the security of liberty and property, and to reduce expenses to what is necessary for the useful purposes of Government.

TH: JEFFERSON.

LETTER TO ROBERT R. LIVINGSTON ON THE
IMPORTANCE OF LOUISIANA AND THE FLORIDAS
April 18, 1802

*In this private letter, carried to the American minister to
France by Du Pont deNemours, is Jefferson's fullest
description of his position on the Mississippi question.
In it he goes considerably farther in threatening an alliance
with England if France took possession of New Orleans
than either he or Secretary of State Madison did in official
correspondence.*

. . . . The cession of Louisiana and the Floridas by Spain to France,
works most sorely on the United States. On this subject the Secretary
of State has written to you full, yet I cannot forbear recurring to it
personally, so deep is the impression it makes on my mind. It completely reverses all the political relations of the United States, and
will form a new epoch in our political course. Of all nations, of any
consideration, France is the one which, hitherto, has offered the few-
est points on which we could have any conflict of right, and the most
points of a communion of interests. From these causes, we have ever
looked to her as our natural friend, as one with which we never could
have an occasion of difference. Her growth, therefore, we viewed as
our own — her misfortunes ours. There is on the globe one single spot,
the possessor of which is our natural and habitual enemy. It is New
Orleans, through which the produced of three-eighths of our territory
must pass to market, and from its fertility it will ere long yield more
than half of our whole produce, and contain more than half of our inhabitants. France, placing herself in that door, assumes to us the
attitude of defiance. Spain might have retained it quietly for years. Her
pacific dispositions, her feeble state, would induce her to increase our
facilities there, so that her possession of the place would be hardly
felt by us, and it would not, perhaps, be very long before some circumstance might arise, which might make the cession of it to us the price
of something of more worth to her. Not so can it ever be in the hands
of France: the impetuosity of her temper, the energy and restlessness
of her character, placed in a point of eternal friction with us, and our
character, which, though quiet and loving peace and the pursuit of
wealth, is high-minded, despising wealth in competition with insult or
injury, enterprising and energetic as any nation on earth; these circumstances render it impossible that France and the United States can
continue long friends, when they meet in so irritable a position. They,
as well as we, must be blind if they do not see this; and we must be
very improvident if we do not begin to make arrangements on that hy-
pothesis. The day that France takes possession of New Orleans, fixes
the sentence which is to restrain her forever within her low-water
mark. It seals the union of two nations, who, in conjunction, can maintain exclusive possession of the ocean. From that moment we must

marry ourselves to the British fleet and nation. We must turn all our attentions to a maritime force, for which our resources place us on very high ground: and having formed and connected together a power which may render reinforcement of her settlements here impossible to France, make the first cannon which shall be fired in Europe the signal for tearing up any settlement she may have made, and for holding the two continents of America in sequestration for the common purposes of the United British and American nations. This is not a state of things we seek or desire. It is one which this measure, if adopted by France, forces on us, as necessarily as any other cause, by the laws of nature, brings on its necessary effect. It is not from a fear of France that we deprecate this measure proposed by her. For however greater her force is than ours, compared in the abstract, it is nothing in comparison of ours, when to be exerted on our soil. But it is from a sincere love of peace, and a firm persuasion, that bound to France by the interests and the strong sympathies still existing in the minds of our citizens, and holding relative positions which insure their continuance, we are secure of a long course of peace. Whereas, the change of friends, which will be rendered necessary if France changes that position, embarks us necessarily as a belligerent power in the first war of Europe. In that case, France will have held possession of New Orleans during the interval of a peace, long or short, at the end of which it will be wrested from her. Will this short-lived possession have been an equivalent to her for the transfer of such a weight into the scale of her enemy? Will not the amalgamation of a young, thriving nation, continue to that enemy the health and force which are at present so evidently on the decline? And will a few years' possession of New Orleans add equally to the strength of France? She may say she needs Louisiana for the supply of her West Indies. She does not need it in time of peace, and in war she could not depend on them, because they would be so easily intercepted. I should suppose that all these considerations might, in some proper form, be brought into view of the government of France. Though stated by us, it ought not to give offence; because we do not bring them forward as a menace, but as counsequences not controllable by us, but inevitable from the course of things. We mention them, not as things which we desire by any means, but as things we deprecate; and we beseech a friend to look forward and to prevent them for our common interests.

If France considers Louisiana, however, as indispensable for her views, she might perhaps be willing to look about for arrangements which might reconceil it to our interests. If anything could do this, it would be the ceding to us the island of New Orleans and the Floridas. This would certainly, in a great degree, remove the causes of jarring and irritation between us, and perhaps for such a length of time as might produce other means of making the measure permanently conciliatory to our interests and friendships. It would, at any rate, relieve us from the necessity of taking immediate measures for countervailling such an operation by arrangements in another quarter. But still we should consider New Orleans and the Floridas as no equivalent for the risk of a quarrel with France, produced by her vicinage .

I have no doubt you have urged these considerations, on every proper occasion, with the government where you are. They are such as must have effect, if you can find means of producing through relection on them by that government. The idea here is, that the troops sent to St. Domingo, were to proceed to Louisiana after finishing their work in that island. If this were the arrangement, it will give you time to return again and again to the charge. For the conquest of St. Domingo will not be a short work. It will take considerable time, and wear down a great number of soldiers. Every eye in the United States is now fixed on the affairs of Louisiana. Perhaps nothing since the Revolutionary War, has produced more uneasy sensations through the body of the nation. Notwithstanding temporary bickerings have taken place with France, she has still a strong hold on the affections of our citizens generally. I have thought it not amiss, by way of supplement to the letters of the Secretary of State, to write you this private one, to impress you with the importance we affix to this transaction.

DECLARATION TO CHIEF HANDSOME LAKE
November 3, 1802

Jefferson's Indian policy was to replace those within our borders with settlers as soon as possible. But he did believe that the Indians owned the land they lived on and should be paid a fair (by Indian standards) price for it. He also believed that the Indians would be better off if they turned from hunting to farming and herding. This statement, one of many similar one he made, expresses his policy briefly.

You remind me, brother, of what I have said to you, when you visited me the last winter, that the lands you then held would remain yours, and should never go from you but when you should be disposed to sell. This I now repeat, and will ever abide by. We, indeed, are always ready to buy land; but we will never ask but when you wish to sell; and our laws, in order to protect you against imposition, have forbidden individuals to purchase lands from you; and have rendered it necessary, when you desire to sell, even to a State, that an agent from the United States should attend the sale, see that your consent is freely given, a satisfactory price paid, and report to us what has been done, for our approbation. This was done in the late case of which you complain. . . .

Nor do I think, brother, that the sale of lands is, under all circumstances, injurious to your people. While they depended on hunting, the more extensive the forrest around them, the more game they would yield. But going into a state of agriculture, it may be as advantageous to a society, as it is to an individual, who has more land than he can improve, to sell a part, and lay out the money in stock and implements of agriculture, for the better improvement of the residue. A little land well stocked and improved, will yield more than a great deal without stock or improvement. I hope, therefore, that on further reflection, you will see this transaction in a more favorable light, both as it concerns the interest of your nation, and the exercise of that superintending care which I am sincerely anxious to employ for their subsistence and happiness. Go on then, brother, in the great reformation you have undertaken. Persuade our red brethren then to be sober, and to cultivate their lands; and their women to spin and weave for their families. You will soon see your women and children well fed and clothed, your men living happily in peace and plenty, and your numbers increasing from year to year. It will be a great glory to you to have been the instrument of so happy a change, and your children's children from generation to generation, will repeat your name with love and gratitude forever. In all your enterprises for the good of your people, you may count with confidence on the aid and protection of the United States, and on the sincerity and zeal with which I am myself animated in the furthering of this humane work. You are our brethren of the same land; we wish your prosperity as brethren should do. Farewell.

SECOND ANNUAL MESSAGE
December 15, 1802

In this paper, Jefferson reported a prosperous nation with few major problems, but only alluded to the most pressing issue: Spain's withdrawal of the right of deposit at New Orleans. On the 22nd, he sent, as requested, all the information he had on the New Orleans situation to the House.

To the Senate and House of Representatives of the United States:

When we assemble together, fellow-citizens, to consider the state of our beloved country, our just attentions are first drawn to those pleasing circumstances which mark the goodness of that Being from whose favor they flow and the large measure of thankfulness we owe for His bounty. Another year has come around, and finds us still blessed with peace and friendship abroad; law, order, and religion at home; both affection and harmony with our Indian neighbors; our burthens lightened, yet our income sufficient for the public wants, and the produce of the year great beyond example. These, fellow-citizens, are the circumstances under which we meet, and we remark with special satisfaction those which under the smiles of Providence result from the skill, industry, and order of our citizens, managing their own affairs in their own way and for their own use, unembarrassed by too much regulation, unoppressed by fiscal exactions.

On the restoration of peace in Europe that portion of the general carrying trade which had fallen to our share during the war was abridged by the returning competition of the belligerent powers. This was to be expected, and was just. But in addition we find in some parts of Europe monopolizing discriminations, which in the form of duties tend effectually to prohibit the carrying thither our own produce in our own vessels. From existing amities and a spirit of justice it is hoped that friendly discussion will produce a fair and adequate reciprocity. But should false calcualtions of interest defeat our hope, it rests with the Legislature to decide whether they will meet inequalities abroad with countervailing inequalities at home, or provide for the evil in any other way. . . .

The cession of the Spanish Province of Louisiana to France, which took place in the course of the late war, will, if carried into effect, make a change in the aspect of our foreign relations which will doubtless have just weight in any deliberations of the Legislature connected with that subject. . . .

To cultivate peace and maintain commerce and navigation in all their lawful enterprises; to foster our fisheries as nurseries of navigation and for the nurture of man, and protect the manufactures adapted to our circumstances; to preserve the faith of the nation by an exact discharge of its debts and contracts, expend the public money with the same care and economy we would practice with our own, and impose on our citizens no unnecessary burthens; to keep in all things within the pale of our constitutional powers, and cherish the federal union as the only rock of safety — these, fellow-citizens, are the landmarks by which we are to guide ourselves in all our proceedings. By continuing to make these the rule of our action we shall endear to our countrymen the true principles of their Constitution and promote an union of sentiment and of action equally auspicious to their happiness and safety. On my part, you may count on a cordial concurrence in every measure for the public good and on all the information I possess which may enable you to discharge to advantage the high functions with which you are invested by your country.

TH. JEFFERSON.

LOUISIANA PURCHASE TREATY
April 30, 1803

Napoleon sold Louisiana because he needed money for the impending war with England and also because he knew France could not fight on the Continent and also defend Louisiana against the Americans, who were sure to ally themselves with England as soon as war broke out. The sale more than doubled the size of the United States.

ARTICLE I. Whereas, by the article the third of the treaty concluded at St. Idelfonso, the 9th Vendemiaire, an. 9 (1st October, 1800) between the First Consul of the French Republic and his Catholic Majesty, it was agreed as follows: "His Catholic Majesty promises and engages on his part, to cede to the French Republic, six months after the full and entire execution of the conditions and stipulations herein relative to his royal highness the duke of Parma, the colony or province of Louisiana, with the same extent that it now has in the hands of Spain, and that it had when France possessed it; and such as it should be after the treaties subsequently entered into between Spain and other states." And whereas, in pursuance of the treaty, and particularly of the third article, the French Republic has an incontestible title to the domain and to the possession of the said territory: The First Consul of the French Republic desiring to give to the United States, in the name of the French Republic, forever and in full sovereignty, the said territory with all its rights and appurtenances, as fully and in the same manner as they have been acquired by the French Republic, in virtue of the above-mentioned treaty, concluded with his Catholic Majesty.

ART. II. In the cession made by the preceding article are included the adjacent islands belonging to Lousiana, all public lots and squares, vacant lands, and all public buildings, fortifications, barracks, and other edifices which are not private property. — The archives, papers, and documents, relative to the domain and sovereignty of Louisiana, and its dependencies, will be left in the possession of the commissaries of the United States, and copies will be afterwards given in due form to the magistrates and municipal officers, of such of the said papers and documents as may be necessary to them.

ART. III. The inhabitants of the ceded territory shall be incorporated in the Union of the United States, and admitted as soon as possible, according to the principles of the Federal constitution, to the enjoyment of all the rights, advantages and immunities of citizens of the United States; and in the mean time they shall be maintained and protected in the free enjoyment of their liberty, property, and the religion which they profess. . . .

ART. V. Immediately after the ratification of the present treaty by the President of the United States, and in case that of the First Consul shall have been previously obtained, the commissary of the French Republic shall remit all the military posts of New Orleans, and other parts of the ceded territory, to the commissary or commissaries named by the President to take possession; the troops, whether of France or Spain, who may be there, shall cease to occupy any military post from the time of taking possession, and shall be embarked, as soon as possible, in the course of three months after the ratification of this treaty. . . .

THIRD ANNUAL MESSAGE
October 17, 1803

*Congress met early to approve the Louisiana Purchase
Treaty and the enabling acts needed to put it into effect.
Jefferson's annual message revealed that no new taxes
were needed to pay for it.*

To the Senate and House of Representatives of the United States:

In calling you together, fellow-citizens, at an earlier day than was
contemplated by the act of the last session of Congress, I have not
been insensible to the personal inconveniences necessarily resulting
from an unexpected change in your arrangements. But matters of
great public concernment have rendered this call necessary, and the
interests you feel in these will supersede in your minds all private
considerations.

Congress witnessed at their late session the extraordinary agitation produced in the public mind by the suspension of our right of
deposit at the port of New Orleans, no assignment of another place
having been made according to treaty. They were sensible that the
continuance of that privation would be more injurious to our nation
than any consequences which could flow from any mode of redress,
but reposing just confidence in the good faith of the Government whose
officer had committed the wrong, friendly and reasonable representations were resorted to, and the right of deposit was restored.

Previous, however, to this period we had not been unaware of the
danger to which our peace would be perpetually exposed whilst so important a key to the commerce of the Western country remained under
foreign power. Difficulties, too, were presenting themselves as to the
navigation of other streams which, arising within our territories, pass
through those adjacent. Propositions had therefore been authorized for
obtaining on fair conditions the sovereignty of New Orleans and of other
possessions in that quarter interesting to our quiet to such extent as
was deemed practicable, and the provisional appropriation of $2,000,000
to be applied and accounted for by the President of the United States,
intended as part of the price, was considered as conveying the sanction
of Congress to the acquisition proposed. The enlightened Government
of France saw with just discernment the importance to both nations of
such liberal arrangements as might best and permanently promote the
peace, friendship, and interests of both, and the property and sovereignty of all Louisiana which had been restored to them have on certain
conditions been trasferred to the United States by instruments bearing
date the 30th of April last. When these shall have received the constitutional sanction of the Senate, they will without delay be communicated
to the Representatives also for the exercise of their functions as to
those conditions which are within the powers vested by the Constitution
in Congress.

Whilst the property and sovereignty of the Mississippi and its waters secure an independent outlet for the produce of the Western States and an uncontrolled navigation through their whole course, free from collision with other powers and the dangers to our peace from that source, the fertility of the country, its climate and extent, promise in due season important aids to our Treasury, an ample provision for our posterity, and a wide spread for the blessings of freedom and equal laws.

With the wisdom of Congress it will rest to take those ulterior measures which may be necessary for the immediate occupation and temporary government of the country; for its incorporation into our Union; for rendering the change of government a blessing to our newly adopted brethren; for securing to them the rights of conscience and of property; for confirming to the Indian inhabitants their occupancy and self government, establishing friendly and commercial relations with them, and for ascertaining the geography of the country acquired. Such materials, for your information, relative to its affairs in general as the short space of time has permitted me to collect will be laid before you when the subject shall be in a state for your consideration. . . .

Should the acquisition of Louisiana be constitutionally confirmed and carried into effect, a sum of nearly $13,000,000 will then be added to our public debt, most of which is payable after fifteen years, before which term the present existing debts will all be discharged by the established operation of the sinking fund. When we contemplate the ordinary annual augmentation of impost from increasing population and wealth, the augmentation of the same revenue by its extension to the new acquisition, and the economies which may still be introduced into our public expenditures, I can not but hope that Congress in reviewing their resources will find means to meet the intermediate interest of this additional debt without recurring to new taxes, and applying to this object only the ordinary progression of our revenue. Its extraordinary increase in times of foreign war will be the proper and sufficient fund for any measures of safety or precaution which that state of things may render necessary in our neutral position. . . .

TH. JEFFERSON

FOURTH ANNUAL MESSAGE
November 8, 1804

Jefferson sent this message in the midst of the presidential election, which he knew he would win although he did not anticipate the resounding landslide. His message told of interference with American shipping by European belligerents, and of progress in Louisiana.

To the Senate and House of Representatives of the United States:

To a people, fellow-citizens, who sincerely desire the happiness and prosperity of other nations; to those who justly calculate that their own well-being is advanced by that of the nations with which they have intercourse, it will be a satisfaction to observe that the war which was lighted up in Europe a little before our last meeting has not yet extended its flames to other nations, nor been marked by the calamities which sometimes stain the footsteps of war. The irregularities, too, on the ocean, which generally harass the commerce of neutral nations, have, in distant parts, disturbed ours less than on former occasions; but in the American seas they have been greater from peculiar causes, and even within our harbors and jurisdiction infringements on the authority of the laws have been committed which have called for serious attention. The friendly conduct of the Governments from whose officers and subjects these acts have proceeded, in other respects and in places more under their observation and control, gives us confidence that our representations on this subject will have been properly regarded.

While noticing the irregularities committed on the ocean by others, those on our own part should not be omitted nor left unprovided for. Complaints have been received that persons residing within the United States have taken on themselves to arm merchant vessels and to force a commerce into certain ports and countries in defiance of the laws of those countries. That individuals should undertake to wage private war, independently of the authority of their country, can not be permitted in a well-ordered society. Its tendency to produce aggression on the laws and rights of other nations and to endanger the peace of our own is so obvious that I doubt not you will adopt measures for restraining it effectually in future.

Soon after the passage of the act of the last session authorizing the establishment of a district and port of entry on the waters of the Mobile we learnt that its object was misunderstood on the part of Spain. Candid explanations were immediately given and assurances that, reserving our claims in that quarter as a subject of discussion and arrangement with Spain, no act was meditated in the meantime inconsistent with the peace and friendship existing between the two nations, and that conformably to these intentions would be the execution of the law. That Government had, however, thought proper to suspend the ratification of the convention of 1802; but the explanations which would reach them soon after, and still more the confirmation of them by the tenor of the instrument establishing the port and district, may reasonably be expected to replace them in the dispositions and views of the whole subject which originally dictated the convention.

I have the satisfaction to inform you that the objections which had been urged by that Government against the validity of our title to the country of Louisiana have been withdrawn, its exact limits, however, remaining still to be settled between us; and to this is to be added that, having prepared and delivered the stock created in execution of the convention of Paris of April 30, 1803, in consideration of the cession of that country, we have received from the Government of France an acknowledgment, in due form, of the fulfillment of that stipulation. . . .

Peace and intercourse with the other powers on the same coast continue on the footing on which they are established by treaty.

In pursuance of the act providing for the temporary government of Louisiana, the necessary officers for the Territory of Orleans were appointed in due time to commence the exercise of their functions on the 1st day of October. The distance, however, of some of them and indispensable previous arrangements may have retarded its commencement in some of its parts. The form of government thus provided having been considered but as temporary, and open to such future improvements as further information of the circumstances of our brethren there might suggest, it will of course be subject to your consideration.

In the district of Louisiana it has been thought best to adopt the division into subordinate districts which had been established under its former government. These being five in number, a commanding officer has been appointed to each, according to the provisions of the law, and so soon as they can be at their stations that district will also be in its due state of organization. In the meantime their places are supplied by the officers before commanding there. And the functions of the governor and judges of Indiana having commenced, the government, we presume, is proceeding in its new form. The lead mines in that district offer so rich a supply of that metal as to merit attention. The report now communicated will inform you of their state and of the necessity of immediate inquiry into their occupation and titles. . . .

TH. JEFFERSON

SECOND INAUGURAL ADDRESS
March 4, 1805

*This address was longer and less ornate than the one Jef-
ferson delivered four years earlier. Then the nation had
emerged from a bitter confrontation, and Jefferson's speech
was conciliatory. This time he had won a resounding vic-
tory and spoke of the success of his policies and the failure of the Federalist's slander campaign.*

Proceeding, fellow-citizens, to that qualification which the Constitution requires before my entrace on the charge again conferred on me,
it is my duty to express the deep sense I entertain of this new proof of
confidence from my fellow-citizens at large, and the zeal with which it
inspires me so to conduct myself as may best satisfy their just ex-
pectations.

On taking this station on a former occasion I declared the principles on which I believed it my duty to administer the affairs of our
Commonwealth. My conscience tells me I have on every occasion
acted up to that declaration according to its obvious import and to the
understanding of every candid mind.

In the transaction of your foreign affairs we have endeavored to
cultivate the friendship of all nations, and especially of those with which
we have the most important relations. We have done them justice on
all occasions, favored where favor was lawful, and cherished mutual
interests and intercourse on fair and equal terms. We are firmly con-
vinced, and we act on that conviction, that with nations as with individuals our interests soundly calculated will ever be found inseparable
from our moral duties, and history bears witness to the fact that a
just nation is trusted on its word when recourse is had to armaments
and wars to bridle others.

At home, fellow-citizens, you best know whether we have done well
or ill. The suppression of unnecessary offices, of useless establishments and expenses, enabled us to discontinue our internal taxes.
These, covering our land with officers and opening our doors to their
intrusions, had already begun that process of domiciliary vexation
which once entered is scarcely to be restrained from reaching suc-
cessively every article of property and produce. If among these taxes
some minor ones fell which had not been inconvenient, it was because
their amount would not have paid the officers who collected them, and
because, if they had any merit, the State authorities might adopt them
instead of others less approved.

The remaining revenue on the consumption of foreign articles is paid
chiefly by those who can afford to add foreign luxuries to domestic

comforts, being collected on our seaboard and frontiers only, and, incorporated with the transactions of our mercantile citizens, it may be
the pleasure and the pride of an American to ask, What farmer, what
mechanic, what laborer ever sees a taxgatherer of the United States?
These contributions enable us to support the current expenses of the
Government, to fulfill contracts with foreign nations, to extinguish the
native right of soil within our limits, to extend those limits, and to apply
such a surplus to our public debts as places at a short day their final
redemption, and that redemption once effected the revenue thereby
liberated may, by a just repartition of it among the States and a cor-
responding amendment of the Constitution, be applied in time of peace
to rivers, canals, roads, arts, manufactures, education, and other great
objects within each State. In time of war, if injustice by ourselves or
others must sometimes produce war, increased as the same revenue
will be by increased population and consumption, and aided by other
resources reserved for that crisis, it may meet within the year all the
expenses of the year without encroaching on the rights of future gener-
ations by burthening them with the debts of the past. War will then be
but a suspension of useful works, and a return to a state of peace a
return to the progress of improvement.

I have said, fellow-citizens, that the income reserved had enabled
us to extend our limits, but that extension may possibly pay for itself
before we are called on, and in the meantime may keep down the accru-
ing interest; in all events, it will replace the advances we shall have
made. I know that the acquisition of Louisiana has been disapproved by
some from a candid apprehension that the enlargement of our territory
would endanger its union. But who can limit the extent to which the
federative principle may operate effectively? The larger our associa-
tion the less will it be shaken by local passions; and in any view is it
not better that the opposite bank of the Mississippi should be settled
by our own brethren and children than by strangers of another family?
With which should we be most likely to live in harmony and friendly
intercourse?

In matters of religion I have considered that its free exercise is
placed by the Constitution independent of the powers of the General Government. I have therefore undertaken on no occasion to prescribe the
religious exercises suited to it, but have left them, as the Constituion
found them, under the direction and discipline of the church or state
authorities acknowledged by the several religious societies.

The aboriginal inhabitants of these countries I have regarded with
the commiseration their history inspires. Endowed with the faculties
and the rights of men, breathing an ardent love of liberty and independence, and occupying a country which left them no desire but to be undisturbed, the stream of overflowing population from other regions
directed itself on these shores; without power to divert or habits to
contend against it, they have been overwhelmed by the current or driven

before it; now reduced within limits too narrow for the hunter's state, humanity enjoins us to teach them agriculture and the domestic arts; to encourage them to that industry which alone can enable them to maintain their place in existence and to prepare them in time for that state of society which to bodily comforts adds the improvement of the mind and morals. We have therefore liberally furnished them with the implements of husbandry and household use; we have placed among them instructors in the arts of first necessity, and they are covered with the aegis of the law against aggressors from among ourselves.

But the endeavors to enlighten them on the fate which awaits their present course of life, to induce them to exercise their reason, follow its dictates, and change their pursuits with the change of circumstances have powerful obstacles to encounter; they are combated by the habits of their bodies, prejudices of their minds, ignorance, pride, and the influence of interested and crafty individuals among them who feel themselves something in the present order of things and fear to become nothing in any other. These persons inculcate a sanctimonious reverence for the customs of their ancestors; that whatsoever they did must be done through all time; that reason is a false guide, and to advance under its counsel in their physical, moral, or political condition is perilous innovation; that their duty is to remain as their Creator made them, ignorance being safety and knowledge full of danger; in short, my friends, among them also is seen the action and counteraction of good sense and of bigotry; they too have their antiphilosophists who find an interest in keeping things in their present state, who dread reformation, and exert all their faculties to maintain the ascendency of habit over the duty of improving our reason and obeying its mandates.

In giving these outlines I do not mean, fellow-citizens, to arrogate to myself the merit of the measures. That is due, in the first place, to the reflecting character of our citizens at large, who, by the weight of public opinion, influence and strengthen the public measures. It is due to the sound discretion with which they select from among themselves those to whom they confide the legislative duties. It is due to the zeal and wisdom of the characters thus selected, who lay the foundations of public happiness in wholesome laws, the execution of which alone remains for others, and it is due to the able and faithful auxiliaries, whose partriotism has associated them with me in the executive functions.

During this course of administration, and in order to disturb it, the artillery of the press has been leveled against us, charged with whatsoever its licentiousness could devise or dare. These abuses of an institution so important to freedom and science are deeply to be regretted, inasmuch as they tend to lessen its usefulness and to sap its safety. They might, indeed, have been corrected by the wholesome punishments reserved to and provided by the laws of the several States against falsehood and defamation, but public duties more urgent press on the time of public servants, and the offenders have therefore been left to find their punishment in the public indignation.

Nor was it uninteresting to the world that an experiment should be fairly and fully made, whether freedom of discussion, unaided by power, is not sufficient for the propagation and protection of truth — whether a government conducting itself in the true spirit of its constitution, with zeal and purity, and doing no act which it would be unwilling the whole world should witness, can be written down by falsehood and defamation. The experiment has been tried; you have witnessed the scene; our fellow-citizens looked on, cool and collected; they saw the latent source from which these outrages proceeded; they gathered around their public functionaries, and when the Constitution called them to the decision by suffrage, they pronounced their verdict, honorable to those who had served them and consolatory to the friend of man who believes that he may be trusted with the control of his own affairs.

No inference is here intended that the laws provided by the States against false and defamatory publications should not be enforced; he who has time renders a service to public morals and public tranquility in reforming these abuses by the salutary coercions of the law; but the experiment is noted to prove that, since truth and reason have maintained their ground against false opinions in league with false facts, the press, confined to truth, needs no other legal restraint; the public judgment will correct false reasonings and opinions on a full hearing of all parties; and no other definite line can be drawn between the inestimable liberty of the press and its demoralizing licentiousness. If there be still improprieties which this rule would not restrain, its supplement must be sought in the censorship of the public opinion.

Contemplating the union of sentiment now manifested so generally as auguring harmony and happiness to our future course, I offer to our country sincere congratulations. With those, too, not yet rallied to the same point the disposition to do so is gaining strength; facts are piercing through the veil drawn over them, and our doubting brethren will at length see that the mass of their fellow-citizens with whom they can not yet resolve to act as to principles and measures, think as they think and desire what they desire; that our wish as well as theirs is that the public efforts may be directed honestly to the public good, that peace be cultivated, civil and religious liberty unassailed, law and order preserved, equality of rights maintained, and state of property, equal or unequal, which results to every man from his own industry or that of his father's. When satisfied of these views it is not in human nature that they should not approve and support them. In the meantime let us cherish them with patient affection, let us do them justice, and more than justice, in all competitions of interest, and we need not doubt that truth, reason, and their own interests will at length prevail, will gather them into the fold of their country, and will

complete that entire union of opinion which gives to a nation the blessing of harmony and the benefit of all its strength.

I shall now enter on the duties to which my fellow-citizens have
again called me, and shall proceed in the spirit of those principles
which they have approved. I fear not that any motives of interest may
lead me astray, I am sensible of no passion which could seduce me
knowlingly from the path of justice, but the weaknesses of human nature
and the limits of my own understanding will produce errors of judgment sometimes injurious to your interests. I shall need, therefore,
all the indulgence which I have heretofore experienced from my con-
stitutents; the want of it will certainly not lessen with increasing
years. I shall need, too, the favor of that Being in whose hands we
are, who led our fathers, as Israel of old, from their native land and
planted them in a country flowing with all the necessaries and comforts of life; who has covered our infancy with His providence and our
riper years with His wisdom and power, and to whose goodness I ask
you to join in supplications with me that He will so enlighten the minds
of your servants, guide their councils, and prosper their measures
that whatsoever they do shall result in your good, and shall secure to
you the peace, friendship, and approbation of all nations.

FIFTH ANNUAL MESSAGE
December 3, 1805

This message told of orderly domestic progress but also of increasing interference with our shipping and asked for measures to strengthen our coastal defenses.

. . . Since our last meeting the aspect of our foreign relations has considerably changed. Our coasts have been infested and our harbors watched by private armed vessels, some of them without commissions, some with illegal commissions, others with those of legal form, but committing piratical acts beyond the authority of their commissions. They have captured in the very entrance of our harbors, as well as on the high seas, not only the vessels of our friends coming to trade with us, but our own also. They have carried them off under pretense of legal adjudication, but not daring to approach a court of justice, they have plundered and sunk them by the way or in obscure places where no evidence could arise against them, maltreated the crews, and abandoned them in boats in the open sea or on desert shores without food or covering. These enormities appearing to be unreached by any control of their sovereigns, I found it necessary to equip a force to cruise within our own seas, to arrest all vessels of these descriptions found hovering on our coasts within the limits of the Gulf Stream and to bring the offenders in for trial as pirates.

The same system of hovering on our coasts and harbors under color of seeking enemies has been also carried on by public armed ships to the great annoyance and oppression of our commerce. New principles, too, have been interpolated into the law of nations, founded neither in justice nor the usage or acknowledgment of nations. According to these a belligerent takes to itself a commerce with its own enemy which it denies to a neutral on the ground of its aiding that enemy in the war; but reason revolts at such an inconsistency, and the neutral having equal right with the belligerent to decide the question, the interests of our constituents and the duty of maintaining the authority of reason, the only umpire between just nations, impose on us the obligation of providing an effectual and determined opposition to a doctrine so injurious to the rights of peaceable nations. Indeed, the confidence we ought to have in the justice of others still countenances the hope that a sounder view of those rights will of itself induce from every belligerent a more correct observance of them.

With Spain our negotiations for a settlement of differences have not had a satisfactory issue. Spoliations during a former war, for which she had formally acknowledged herself responsible, have been refused to be compensated but on conditions affecting other claims in no wise connected with them. Yet the same practices are renewed in the present war and are alrady of great amount. On the Mobile, our commerce passing through that river continues to be obstructed by arbitrary duties and vexatious searches. Propositions for adjusting amicably the boundaries of Lousiana have not been acceded to. While, however, the right is unsettled, we have avoided changing the state of things by taking new posts or strengthening ourselves in the disputed territories, in the hope that the other power would not by a contrary conduct oblige us to meet their example and endanger conflicts of authority the issue of which may not be easily controlled. But in this hope we have now reason to lessen our confidence. Inroads have been recently made into the Territories of Orleans and the Mississippi, our citizens have been seized and their property plundered in the very parts of the former which had been actually delivered up by Spain, and this by the regular officers and soldiers of that Government. I have therefore found it necessary at length to give orders to our troops on that frontier to be in readiness to protect our citizens, and to repel by arms any similar aggressions in future. Other details necessary for your full information of the state of things between this country and that shall be the subject of another communication.

In reviewing these injuries from some of the belligerent powers the moderation, the firmness, and the wisdom of the Legislature will all be called into action. We ought still to hope that time and a more correct estimate of interest as well as of character will produce the justice we are bound to expect. But should any nation deceive itself by false calculations, and disappoint that expectation, we must join in the unprofitable contest of trying which party can do the other the most harm. Some of these injuries may perhaps admit a peaceable remedy. Where that is competent it is always the most desirable. But some of them are of a nature to be met by force only, and all of them may lead to it. I can not, therefore, but recommend such preparations as circumstances call for. The first object is to place our seaport towns out of the danger of insult. Measures have been already taken for furnishing them with heavy cannon for the service of such land batteries as may make a part of their defense against armed vessels approaching them. In aid of these it is desirable we should have a competent number of gunboats, and the number, to be competent, must be considerable. If immediately begun, they may be in readiness for service at the opening of the next season. Whether it will be necessary to augment our land forces will be decided by occurrences probably in the course of your session. In the meantime you will consider whether it would not be expedient for a state of peace as well as of war so to organize or class the militia as would enable us on any sudden emergency to call for the services of the younger portions, unencumbered with the old and those having families. Upward of 300,000 able-bodied men between the ages of 18 and 26 years, which the last census shews we may now count within our limits, will furnish a competent number for offense or defense in any point where they may be wanted, and will give time for raising regular forces after the necessity of them shall become certain; and the reducing to the early period of life all its active service can not but be desirable to our younger citizens of the present as well as future times, inasmuch as it engages to them in more advanced age a quiet and undisturbed repose in the bosom of their families. I can not, then, but earnestly recommend to your early consideration the expediency of so modifying our militia system as, by a separation of the more active part from that which is less so, we may draw from it when necessary an efficient corps fit for real and active service, and to be called to it in regular rotation.

Considerable provision has been made under former authorities from Congress of materials for the construction of ships of war of 74 guns. These materials are on hand subject to the further will of the Legislature. . . .

                                                    TH. JEFFERSON

PROCLAMATION ON BURR'S PLOT
November 27, 1806

*Jefferson had heard reports of Burr's plotting a revolution
in the west as early as the winter of 1805-06, but he chose
to rely on the loyalty of the western population rather than
take steps against the plot. But rumors became more in-
sistent through the spring and summer of 1806. Finally,
Jefferson received a letter from a disenchanted conspira-
tor, General James Wilkinson, commander of the army in
New Orleans, telling of the plot. Two days later, Jefferson
issued this proclamation.*

Whereas information has been received that sundry persons, citizens of the United States or residents within the same, are conspiring
and confederating together to begin and set on foot, provide, and prepare the means for a military expedition or enterprise against the
dominions of Spain; that for this purpose they are fitting out and arming vessels in the western waters of the United States, collecting provisions, arms, military stores, and means; are deceiving and seducing
honest and well-meaning citizens, under various pretenses, to engage
in their criminal enterprises; are organizing, officering, and arming
themselves for the same, contrary to the laws in such cases made and
provided:

I have therefore thought proper to issue this my proclamation,
warning and enjoining all faithful citizens who have been led without
due knowledge or consideration to participate in the said unlawful
enterprises to withdraw from the same without delay, and commanding
all persons whatsoever engaged or concerned in the same to cease all
further proceedings therein, as they will answer the contrary at their
peril and incur prosecution with all the rigors of the law. And I hereby
enjoin and require all officers, civil and military, of the United States,
or of any of the States or Territories, and especially all governors
and other executive authorities, all judges, justices, and other officers
of the peace, all military officers of the Army or Navy of the United
States, or officers of the militia, to be vigilant, each within his respective department and according to his functions, in searching out and
bringing to condign punishment all persons engaged or concerned in
such enterprise, in seizing and detaining, subject to the disposition
of the law, all vessels, arms, military stores, or other means provided
or providing for the same, and, in general, in preventing the carrying
on such expedition or enterprise by all lawful means within their power;
and I require all good and faithful citizens and others within the United
States to be aiding and assisting herein, and especially in the discovery,
apprehension, and bringing to justice of all such offenders, in prevent-

ing the execution of their unlawful designs, and in giving information against them to the proper authorities.

In testimony whereof I have caused the seal of the United States to be affixed to these presents, and have signed the same with my hand.

Given at the city of Washington on the 27th day of November, 1806, and in the year of the Sovereignty of the United States the thirty-first.

TH. JEFFERSON

By the President:
        JAMES MADISON,
            Secretary of State

SIXTH ANNUAL MESSAGE
December 1, 1806

*In this message, Jefferson wrote of unsettled foreign rela-
tions, told of Lewis' and Clark's return from the Pacific,
alluded to Burr's plot, and suggested spending part of the
growing federal surplus for education and other public improvements.*

To the Senate and House of Representatives of the United States of
America in Congress assembled:

It would have given me, fellow-citizens, great satisfaction to announce in the moment of your meeting that the difficulties in our foreign
relations existing at the time of your last separation had been amicably
and justly terminated. I lost no time in taking those measures which
were most likely to bring them to such a termination — by special
missions charged with such powers and instructions as in the event of
failure could leave no imputation on either our moderation or forbearance. The delays which have since taken place in our negotiations
with the British Government appear to have proceeded from causes
which do not forbid the expectation that duing the course of the session
I may be enabled to lay before you their final issue. What will be that
of the negotiations for settling our differences with Spain nothing which
had taken place at the date of the last dispatches enables us to pro-
nounce. . . .

Having received information that in another part of the United
States a great number of private individuals were combinging together, arming and organizing themselves contrary to law, to carry
on a military expedition against the territories of Spain, I thought it
necessary, by proclamation as well as by special orders, to take
measures for preventing and suppressing this enterprise, for seizing
the vessels, arms, and other means provided for it, and for arresting
and bringing to justice its authors and abettors. It was due to that
good faith which ought ever to be the rule of action in public as well
as in private transactions, it was due to good order and regular government, that while the public force was acting strictly on the defensive
and merely to protect our citizens from aggression the criminal attempts of private individuals to decide for their country the question
of peace or war by commencing active and unauthorized hostilities
should be promptly and efficaciously suppressed.

Whether it will be necessary to enlarge our regular force will
depend on the result of our negotiations with Spain; but as it is uncertain when that result will be known, the provisional measures requisite for that, and to meet any pressure intervening in that quarter,
will be a subject for your early consideration. . . .

When both of these branches of revenue shall in this way be relinquished there will still ere long be an accumulation of moneys in the Treasury beyond the installments of public debt which we are permitted by contract to pay. They can not then, without a modification assented to by the public creditors, be applied to the extinguishment of this debt and the complete liberation of our revenues, the most desirable of all objects. Nor, if our peace continues, will they be wanting for any other existing purpose. The question therefore now comes forward, To what other objects shall these surpluses be appropriated, and the whole surplus of impost, after the entire discharge of the public debt, and during those intervals when the purposes of war shall not call for them? Shall we suppress the impost and give that advantage to foreign over domestic manufactures? On a few articles of more general and necessary use the suppression in due season will doubtless be right, but the great mass of the articles on which impost is paid are foreign luxuries, purchased by those only who are rich enough to afford themselves the use of them. Their patriotism would certainly prefer its continuance and application to the great purposes of the public education, roads, rivers, canals, and such other objects of public improvement as it may be thought proper to add to the constitutional enumeration of Federal powers. By these operations new channels of communication will be opened between the States, the lines of separation will disappear, their interests will be identified, and their union cemented by new and indissoluble ties. Education is here placed among the articles of public care, not that it would be proposed to take its ordinary branches out of the hands of private enterprise, which manages so much better all the concerns to which it is equal, but a public institution can alone supply those sciences which though rarely called for are yet necessary to complete the circle, all the parts of which contribute to the improvement of the country and some of them to its preservation. The subject is now proposed for the consideration of Congress, because if approved by the time the State legislatures shall have deliberated on this extension of the Federal trusts, and the laws shall be passed and other arrangements made for their execution, the necessary funds will be on hand and without employment. I suppose an amendment to the Constitution, by consent of the States, necessary, because the objects now recommended are not among those enumerated in the Constitution, and to which it permits the public moneys to be applied.

The present consideration of a national establishment for education particularly is rendered proper by this circumstance also, that if Congress, approving the proposition, shall yet think it more eligible to found it on a donation of lands, they have it now in their power to endow it with those which will be among the earliest to produce the necessary income. This foundation would have the advantage of being independent of war, which may suspend other improvements by requiring for its own purposes the resources destined for them. . . . TH. JEFFERSON

REFUSAL TO OBEY A SUBPOENA
June 20, 1807

*Edmond Randolph and Burr's other attorneys asked Chief
Justice John Marshall, the presiding judge, to issue a sub-
poena to the President to compel him to appear and testify
in Burr's trial. Jefferson had already sent papers relevant
to the proceedings, but he refused to appear personally. He
explained his reasons in a letter to George Hay, the federal prosecuting attorney.*

. . . I did not see till last night the opinion of the judge on the
supaena duces tecum against the President. Considering the question
there as coram non judice, I did not read his argument with much attention. Yet I saw readily enough, that, as is usual where an opinion
is to be supported, right or wrong, he dwells much on smaller objections, and passes over those which are solid. Laying down the position
generally, that all persons owe obedience to subpoenas, he admits no
exception unless it can be produced in his law books. But if the Constitution enjoins on a particular officer to be always engaged in a
particular set of duties imposed on him, does not this supersede the
general law, subjecting him to minor duties inconsistent with these?
The Constitution enjoins his constant agency in the concerns of six
millions of people. Is the law paramount to this, which calls on him on
behalf of a single one? Let us apply the judge's own doctrine to the case
of himself and his brethren. The sheriff of Henrico summons him from
the bench, to quell a riot somewhere in his county. The federal judge
is, by the general law, a part of the posse of the State sheriff. Would
the judge abandon major duties to perform lesser ones? Again; the
court of Orleans or Maine commands, by subpoenas, the attendance of
all the judges of the Supreme Court. Would they abandon their posts
as judges, and the interests of millions committed to them, to serve
the purposes of a single individual? The leading principle of our Constitution is the independence of the legislature, executive and judiciary,
of each other and none are more jealous of this than the judiciary. But
would the executive be independent of the judiciary, if he were subject
to the commands of the latter, and to imprisonment for disobedience;
if the several courts could bandy him from pillar to post, keep him
constantly trudging from north to south and east to west, and withdraw
him entirely from his Constitutional duties? The intention of the Constitution, that each branch should be independent of the others, is
further manifested by the means than to the Executive. . . .

SEVENTH ANNUAL MESSAGE
October 27, 1807

After Congress convened early to consider an anticipated reply from the English on the Chesapeake affair, Jefferson had to report that the negotiators, Monroe and William Pinkney had made no progress. He also wrote of defensive measures he had taken and others that might be necessary.

To the Senate and House of Representatives of the United States:

Circumstances, fellow-citizens, which seriously threatened the peace of our country have made it a duty to convene you at an earlier period than usual. The love of peace so much cherished in the bosoms of our citizens, which has so long guided the proceedings of their public councils and induced forbearance under so many wrongs, may not insure our continuance in the quiet pursuits of industry. The many injuries and depredations committed on our commerce and navigation upon the high seas for years past, the successive innovations on those principles of public law which have been established by the reason and usage of nations as the rule of their intercourse and the umpire and security of their rights and peace, and all the circumstances which induced the extraordinary mission to London are already known to you. The instructions given to our ministers were framed in the sincerest spirit of amity and moderation. They accordingly proceeded, in conformity therewith, to propose arrangements which might embrace and settle all the points in difference between us, which might bring us to a mutual understanding on our neutral and national rights and provide for a commercial intercourse on conditions of some equality. After long and fruitless endeavors to effect the purposes of their mission and to obtain arrangements within the limits of their instructions, they concluded to sign such as could be obtained and to send them for consideration, candidly declaring to the other negotiators at the same time that they were acting against their instructions, and that their Government, therefore, could not be pledged for ratification. Some of the articles proposed might have been admitted on a principle of compromise, but others were too highly disadvantageous, and no sufficient provision was made against the principal source of the irritations and collisions which were constantly endangering the peace of the two nations. The question, therefore, whether a treaty should be accepted in that form could have admitted but of one decision, even had no declarations of the other party impaired our confidence in it. Still anxious not to close the door against friendly adjustment, new modifications were framed and further concessions authorized than could before have been supposed necessary; and our ministers were instructed to resume their negotiations on these grounds. On this new reference to amicable discussion we were reposing in confidence, when on the 22nd day of June last by a formal order from a British admiral the frigate

Chesapeake, leaving her port for a distant service, was attacked by one of the vessels which had been lying in our harbors under the indulgences of hospitality, was disabled from proceeding, had several of her crew killed and four taken away. On this outrage no commentaries are necessary. Its character has been pronounced by the indignant voice of our citizens with an emphasis and unanimity never exceeded. I immediately, by proclamation, interdicted our harbors and waters to all British armed vessels, forbade intercourse with them, and uncertain how far hostilities were intended, and the town of Norfolk, indeed, being threatened with immediate attack, a sufficient force was ordered for the protection of that place, and such other preparations commenced and pursued as the prospect rendered proper. An armed vessel of the United States was dispatched with instructions to our ministers at London to call on that Government for the satisfaction and security required by the outrage. A very short interval ought now to bring the answer, which shall be communicated to you as soon as received; then also, or as soon after as the public interests shall be found to admit, the unratified treaty and proceedings relative to it shall be made known to you.

The aggression thus begun has been continued on the part of the British commanders by remaining within our waters in defiance of the authority of the country, by habitual violations of its jurisdiction, and at length by putting to death one of the persons whom they had forcibly taken from on board the Chesapeake. These aggravations necessarily lead to the policy either of never admitting an armed vessel into our harbors or of maintaining in every harbor such an armed force as may constrain obedience to the laws and protect the lives and property of our citizens against their armed guests; but the expense of such a standing force and its inconsistence with our principles dispense with those courtesies which would necessarily call for it, and leave us equally free to exclude the navy, as we are the army, of a foreign power from entering our limits.

To former violations of maritime rights another is now added of very extensive effect. The Government of that nation has issued an order interdicting all trade by neutrals between ports not in amity with them; and being now at war with nearly every nation on the Atlantic and Mediterranean seas, our vessels are required to sacrifice their cargoes at the first port they touch or to return home without the benefit of going to any other market. Under this new law of the ocean our trade on the Mediterranean has been swept away by seizures and condemnations, and that in other seas is threatened with the same fate. . . .

The appropriations of the last session for the defense of our seaport towns and harbors were made under expectation that a continuance of our peace would permit us to proceed in that work according to our convenience. It has been though better to apply the sums then given toward the defense of New York, Charleston, and New Orleans chiefly, as most open and most likely first to need protection, and to leave places less immediately in danger to the provisions of the present session.

The gunboats, too, already provided have on a like principle been chiefly assigned to New York, New Orleans, and the Chesapeake. Whether our movable force on the water, so material in aid of the defensive works on the land, should be augmented in this or any other form is left to the wisdom of the Legislature. For the purpose of manning these vessels in sudden attacks on our harbors it is a matter for consideration whether the seamen of the United States may not justly be formed into a special militia, to be called on for tours of duty in defense of the harbors where they shall happen to be, the ordinary militia of the place furnishing that portion which may consist of landsmen.

The moment our peace was threatened I deemed it indispensable to secure a greater provision of those articles of military stores with which our magazines were not sufficiently furnished. To have awaited a previous and special sanction by law would have lost occasions which might not be retrieved. I did not hesitate, therefore, to authorize engagements for such supplements to our existing stock as would render it adequate to the emergencies threatening us, and I trust that the Legislature, feeling the same anxiety for the safety of our country, so materially advanced by this precaution, will approve, when done, what they would have seen so important to be done if then assembled. Expenses, also unprovided for, arose out of the necessity of calling all our gunboats into actual service for the defense of our harbors; of all which accounts will be laid before you.

Whether a regular army is to be raised, and to what extent, must depend on the information so shortly expected. In the meantime I have called on the States for quotas of militia, to be in readiness for present defense, and have, moreover, encouraged the acceptance of volunteers; and I am happy to inform you that these have offered themselves with great alacrity in every part of the Union. They are ordered to be organized and ready at a moment's warning to proceed on any service to which they may be called, and every preparation within the Executive powers has been made to insure us the benefit of early exertions. . . .

                                                    TH. JEFFERSON

EMBARGO ACT
December 22, 1807

This act, passed to protect American shipping from con-
fiscation by the English and French, caused economic
havoc, not only in the merchant marine, but also in the
nation as a whole. Farm prices dropped, and many small
businesses were forced into bankruptcy. Smuggling was
widespread, often with no attempt at concealment. Jeffer-
son finally signed the act's repeal and another (the Non-
Intercourse Act) banning trade with England and France
on his last day in office.

Be it enacted . . . , That an embargo be, and hereby is laid on all ships and vessels in the ports and places within the limits or juris-diction of the United States, cleared or not cleared, bound to any foreign port or place; and that no clearance be furnished to any ship or vessel bound to such foreign port or place, except vessels under the immediate direction of the President of the United States; and that the President be authorized to give such instructions to the officers of the revenue, and of the navy and revenue cutters of the United States, as shall appear best adapted for carrying the same into full effect: Provided, that nothing herein contained shall be construed to prevent the departure of any foreign ship or vessel, either in ballast, or with the goods, wares and merchandise on board of such foreign ship or vessel, when notified of this act.

SEC. 2.   And be it further enacted, That during the continuance of this act, no registered, or sea letter vessel, having on board goods, wares and merchandise, shall be allowed to depart from one port of the United States to any other within the same, unless the master, owner, consignee or factor of such vessel shall first give bond, with one or more sureties to the collector of the district from which she is bound to depart, in a sum of double the value of the vessel and cargo, that the said goods, wares, or merchandise shall be relanded in some port of the United States, dangers of the seas excepted, which bond, and also a certificate from the collector where the same may be re-landed, shall by the collector respectively be transmitted to the Sec-retary of the Treasury. All armed vessels possessing public commis-sions from any foreign power, are not to be considered as liable to the embargo laid by this act.

EIGHTH ANNUAL MESSAGE
November 8, 1808

*In his last annual message, Jefferson admitted that the
embargo was a failure but said the only alternative was
war, not submission to England's and France's treatment
of American ships. He also spoke of defensive measures
and pointed to his reduction of the national debt while in
office.*

To the Senate and House of Representatives of the United States:

It would have been a surce, fellow-citizens, of much gratification
if our last communications from Europe had enabled me to inform
you that the belligerent nations, whose disregard of neutral rights
has been so destructive to our commerce, had become awakened to
the duty and true policy of revoking their unrighteous edicts. That no
means might be omitted to produce this salutary effect, I lost no time
in availing myself of the act authorizing a suspension, in whole or in
part, of the several embargo laws. Our ministers at London and Paris
were instructed to explain to the respective Governments there our
disposition to exercise the authority in such manner as would withdraw
the pretext on which the aggressions were originally founded and open
the way for a renewal of that commercial intercourse which it was
alleged on all sides had been reluctantly obstructed. As each of those
Governments had pledged its readiness to concur in renouncing a measure which reached its adversary through the incontestable rights of
neutrals only, and as the measure had been assumed by each as a re-
taliation for an asserted acquiescence in the aggressions of the other,
it was reasonably expected that the occasion would have been seized
by both for evincing the sincerity of their professions, and for restoring
to the commerce of the United States its legitimate freedom. The instructions to our ministers with respect to the different belligerents
were necessarily modified with a reference to their different circumstances, and to the condition annexed by law to the Executive power of
suspension, requiring a decree of security to our commerce which
would not result from a repeal of the decrees of France. Instead of a
pledge, therefore, of a suspension of the embargo as to her in case
of such a repeal, it was presumed that a sufficient inducement might
be found in other considerations, and particularly in the change produced by a compliance with our just demands by one belligerent and a
refusal by the other in the relations between the other and the United
States. To Great Britain, whose power on the ocean is so ascendant,
it was deemed not inconsistent with that condition to state explicitly
that on her rescinding her orders in relation to the United States their
trade would be opened with her, and remain shut to her enemy in case
of his failure to rescind his decrees also. From France no answer

has been received, nor any indication that the requisite change in her decrees is contemplated. The favorable reception of the proposition to Great Britain was the less to be doubted, as her orders of council had not only been referred for their vindication to an acquiescence on the part of the United States no longer to be pretended, but as the arrangement proposed, whilst it resisted the illegal decrees of France, involved, moreover, substantially the precise advantages professedly aimed at by the British orders. The arrangement has nevertheless been rejected.

This candid and liberal experiment having thus failed, and no other event having occurred on which a suspension of the embargo by the Executive was authroized, it necessarily remains in the extent originally given to it. We have the satisfaction, however, to reflect that in return for the privations imposed by the measure, and which our fellow-citizens in general have borne with patriotism, it has had the important effects of saving our mariners and our vast mercantile property, as well as of affording time for prosecuting the defensive and provisional measures called for by the occasion. It has demonstrated to foreign nations the moderation and firmness which govern our councils, and to our citizens the necessity of uniting in support of the laws and the rights of their country, and has thus long frustrated those usurpations and spoliations which, if resisted, involved war; if submitted to, sacrificed a vital principle of our national independence.

Under a continuance of the belligerent measures which, in defiance of laws which consecrate the rights of neutrals, overspread the ocean with danger, it will rest with the wisdom of Congress to decide on the course best adapted to such a state of things; and bringing with them, as they do, from every part of the Union the sentiments of our constituents, my confidence is strengthened that in forming this decision they will, with an unerring regard to the essential rights and interests of the nation, weigh and compare the painful alternatives out of which a choice is to be made. Nor should I do justice to the virtues which on other occasions have marked the character of our fellow-citizens if I did not cherish an equal confidence that the alternative chosen, whatever it may be, will be maintained with all the fortitude and patriotism which the crisis ought to inspire.

The documents containing the correspondences on the subject of the foreign edicts against our commerce, with the instructions given to our ministers at London and Paris, are now laid before you.

The communications made to Congress at their last session explained the posture in which the close of the discussions relating to the attack by a British ship of war on the frigate Chesapeake left a subject on which the nation had manifested so honorable a sensibility. Every view of what had passed authorized a belief that immediate steps would be taken by the British Government for redressing a wrong which the more it was investigated appeared the more clearly

to require what had not been provided for in the special mission. It is found that no steps have been taken for the purpose. On the contrary, it will be seen in the documents laid before you that the inadmissible preliminary which obstructed the adjustment is still adhered to, and, moreover, that it is now brought into connection with the distinct and irrelative case of the orders in council. The instructions which had been given to our minister at London with a view to facilitate, if necessary, the reparation claimed by the United States are included in the documents communicated.

Our relations with the other powers of Europe have undergone no material changes since your last session. The important negotiations with Spain which had been alternately suspended and resumed necessarily experience a pause under the extraordinary and interesting crisis which distinguishes her internal situation.

With the Barbary Powers we continue in harmony, with the exception of an unjustifiable proceeding of the Dey of Algiers toward our consul to that Regency. Its character and circumstances are now laid before you, and will enable you to decide how far it may, either now or hereafter, call for any measures not within the limits of the Executive authority.

With our Indian neighbors the public peace has been steadily maintained. Some instances of individual wrong have, as at other times, taken place, but in no wise implicating the will of the nation. Beyond the Mississippi the Ioways, the Sacs, and the Alabamas have delivered up for trial and punishment individuals from among themselves accused of murdering citizens of the United States. On this side of the Mississippi the Creeks are exerting themselves to arrest offenders of the same kind, and the Choctaws have manifested their readiness and desire for amicable and just arrangements respecting depredations committed by disorderly persons of their tribe. And, generally, from a conviction that we consider them as a part of ourselves, and cherish with sincerity their rights and interests, the attachment of the Indian tribes is gaining strength daily – is extending from the nearer to the more remote, and will amply requite us for the justice and friendship practiced toward them. Husbandry and household manufacture are advancing among them more rapidly with the Southern than Northern tribes, from circumstances of soil and climate, and one of the two great divisions of the Cherokee Nation have now under consideration to solicit the citizenship of the United States, and to be identified with us in laws and government in such progressive manner as we shall think best.

In consequence of the appropriations of the last session of Congress for the security of our seaport towns and harbors, such works of defense have been erected as seemed to be called for by the situation of the several places, their relative importance, and the scale of expense indicated by the amount of the appropriation. These works will chiefly be finished in the course of the present season, except at New York and New Orleans, where most was to be done; and although a great proportion of the last appropriation has been expended on the former place, yet some further views will be submitted to Congress for rendering its security entirely adequate against naval enterprise. A view of what has been done at the several places, and of what is proposed to be done, shall be communicated as soon as the several reports are received.

Of the gunboats authorized by the act of December last, it has been thought necessary to build only 103 in the present year. These, with those before possessed, are sufficient for the harbors and waters most exposed, and the residue will require little time for their construction when it shall be deemed necessary.

Under the act of the last session for raising an additional military force so many officers were immediately appointed as were necessary for carrying on the business of recruiting, and in proportion as it advanced others have been added. We have reason to believe their success has been satisfactory, although such returns have not yet been received as enable me to present you a statement of the numbers engaged.

I have not thought it necessary in the course of the last season to call for any general detachments of militia or of volunteers under the laws passed for that purpose. For the ensuing season, however, they will be required to be in readiness should their service be wanted. Some small and special detachments have been necessary to maintain the laws of embargo on that portion of our northern frontier which offered peculiar evasion, but these were replaced as soon as it could be done by bodies of new recruits. By the aid of these and of the armed vessels called into service in other quarters the spirit of disobedience and abuse, which manifested itself early and with sensible effect while we were unprepared to meet it, has been considerably repressed.

Considering the extraordinary character of the times in which we live, our attention should unremittingly be fixed on the safety of our country. For a people who are free, and who mean to remain so, a well organized and armed militia is their best security. It is therefore incumbent on us at every meeting to revise the condition of the militia, and to ask ourselves if it is prepared to repel a powerful enemy at every point of our territories exposed to invasion. Some of the States have paid a laudable attention to this object, but every degree of neglect is to be gound among others. Congress alone having the power to produce an uniform state of preparation in this great organ of defense, the interests which they so deeply feel in their own and their country's security will present this as among the most important objects of their deliberation.

Under the acts of March 11 and April 23 respecting arms, the difficulty of procuring them from abroad during the present situation and dispositions of Europe induced us to direct our whole efforts to the means of internal supply. The public factories have therefore been enlarged, additional machineries erected, and, in proportion as artificers can be found or formed, their effect, already more than doubled, may be increased so as to keep pace with the yearly increase of the militia. The annual sums appropriated by the latter act have been directed to the encouragement of private factories of arms, and contracts have been entered into with individual undertakers to nearly the amount of the first year's appropriation.

The suspension of our foreign commerce, produced by the injustice of the belligerent powers, and the consequent losses and sacrifices of our citizens are subjects of just concern. The situation into which we have thus been forced has impelled us to apply a portion of our industry and capital to internal manufactures and improvements. The extent of this conversion is daily increasing, and little doubt remains that the establishments formed and forming will, under the auspices of cheaper materials and subsistence, the freedom of labor from taxation with us, and of protecting duties and prohibitions, become permanent. The commerce with the Indians, too, within our own boundaries is likely to receive abundant aliment from the same internal source, and will secure to them peace and the progress of civilization, undisturbed by practices hostile to both.

The accounts of the receipts and expenditures during the year ending the 30th of September last being not yet made up, a correct statement will hereafter be transmitted from the Treasury. In the meantime is ascertained that the receipts have amounted to near $18,000,000 which, with the eight millions and a half in the Treasury at the beginning of the year, have enabled us, after meeting the current demands and interest incurred, to pay $2,300,000 of the principal of our funded debt, and left us in the Treasury on that day near $14,000,000. Of these, $5,350,000 will be necessary to pay what will be due on the 1st day of January next, which will complete the reimbursement of the 8 per cent stock. These payments, with those made in the six years and a half preceding, will have extinguished $33,580,000 of the principal of the funded debt, being the whole which could be paid or purchased within the limits of the law and of our contracts, and the amount of principal thus discharged will have liberated the revenue from about $2,000,000 of interest and added that sum annually to the disposable surplus. The probable accumulation of the surpluses of revenue beyond what can be applied to the payment of the public debt whenever the freedom and safety of our commerce shall be restored merits the consideration of Congress. Shall it lie unproductive in the public vaults? Shall the revenue be reduced? Or shall it not rather be appropriated to the improvements of roads, canals, rivers, education, and other great foundations of prosperity and union under the powers which Congress may already possess or such amendment of the Constitution as may be approved by the States? While uncertain of the course of things, the time may be advantageously employed in obtaining the powers necessary for a system of improvement, should that be thought best.

Availing myself of this the last occasion which will occur of addressing the two Houses of the Legislature at their meeting, I can not omit the expression of my sincere gratitude for the repeated proofs of confidence manifested to me by themselves and their predecessors since my call to the administration and the many indulgences experienced at their hands. The same grateful acknowledgment under all embarrassments. In the transaction of their business I can not have escaped error. It is incident to our imperfect nature. But I may say with truth my errors have been of the understanding, not of intention, and that the advancement of their rights and interests has been the constant motive for every measure. On these considerations I solicit their indulgence. Looking forward with anxiety to their future destines, I trust that in their steady character, unshaken by difficulties, in their love of liberty, obedience to law, and support of the public authorities I see a sure guaranty of the permanence of our Republic; and, retiring from the charge of their affairs, I carry with me the consolation of a firm persuasion that Heaven has in store for our beloved country long ages to come of prosperity and happiness.

TH. JEFFERSON

LETTER ON SLAVERY
August 25, 1814

Jefferson was opposed to slavery, and felt that slaves should be freed only after they had been taught a trade so they could support themselves. He freed several of his own slaves and wrote provisions banning slavery into his revision of the Virginia laws and into several official papers, only to have them deleted. He discussed the problem in his Notes on Virginia and in many letters to friends over the years. This letter to Edward Coles is a succinct expression of his long-held views.

DEAR SIR: Your favor of July 31 was duly received, and was read with peculiar pleasure. The sentiments breathed through the whole, do honor both to the head and heart of the writer. Mine, on the subject of the slavery of negroes, have long since been in possession of the public, and time has only served to give them stronger proof. The love of justice and the love of country plead equally the cause of these people, and it is a mortal reproach to us that they should have pleaded so long in vain, and should have produced not a single effort, nay, I fear, not much serious willingness to relieve them and ourselves, from our present condition of moral and political reprobation.

From those in a former generation, who were in the fullness of age when I came into public life, which was while our controversy with England was on paper only, I soon saw that nothing was to be hoped. Nursed and educated in the daily habit of seeing the degraded condition, both bodily and mental, of those unfortunate beings, not reflecting that that degradation was very much the work of themselves and their fathers, few minds had yet doubted but that they were as legitimate subjects of property as their horses or cattle. The quiet and monotonous course of colonial life had been disturbed by no alarm, and little reflection on the value of liberty. And when an alarm was taken at an enterprise of their own, it was not easy to carry them the whole length of the principles which they invoked for themselves.

In the first or second session of the legislature, after I became a member, I drew to this subject the attention of Colonel Bland, one of the oldest, ablest, and most respected members, and he undertook to move for certain moderate extensions of the protection of the laws to these people. I seconded his motion, and, as a younger member, was more spared in the debate; but he was denounced as an enemy to his country, and was treated with the greatest indecorum. From an early stage of our Revolution, other and more distant duties were assigned to me, so that from that time till my return from Europe, in 1789, and I may say, till I returned to reside at home in 1809, I had little opportunity of knowing the progress of public sentiment here on this subject.

I had always hoped that the younger generation, receiving their early impressions after the flame of liberty had been kindled in every breast, and had become, as it were, the vital spirit of every American, that the generous temperament of youth, analogous to the motion of their blood, and above the suggestions of avarice, would have sympathized with oppression wherever found, and proved their love of liberty beyond their own share of it. But my intercourse with them, since my return, has not been sufficient to ascertain that they had made towards this point the progress I had hoped.

Your solitary but welcome voice is the first which has brought this sound to my ear; and I have considered the general silence which prevails on this subject, as indicating an apathy unfavorable to every hope. Yet the hour of emancipation is advancing in the march of time. It will come; and whether brought on by the generous energy of our own minds, or by the bloody process of St. Domingo, excited and conducted by the power of our present enemy, if once stationed permanently within our country, and offering asylum and arms to the oppressed, is a leaf of our history not yet turned over.

As to the method by which this difficult work is to be effected, if permitted to be done by ourselves. I have seen no proposition so expedient, on the whole, as that of emancipation of those born after a given day, and of their education and expatriation at a proper age. This would give time for a gradual extinction of that species of labor, and substition of another, and lessen the severity of the shock, which an operation so fundamental cannot fail to produce. The idea of emancipating the whole at once, the old as well as the young, and retaining them here, is of those only who have not the guide of either knowledge or experience on the subject. For men, probably of any color, but of this color we know, brought up from their infancy without necessity for thought or forecast, are by their habits rendered as incapable as children of taking care of themselves, and are extinguished promptly wherever industry is necessary for raising the young. In the meantime, they are pests in society by their idleness, and the depredations to which this leads them. Their amalgamation with the other color produces a degradation to which no lover of his country, no lover of excellence in the human character, can innocently consent.

I am sensible of the partialities with which you have looked towards me as the person who should undertake this salutary but arduous work. But this, my dear sir, is like bidding old Priam to buckle on the armor of Hector — "trementibus aevo humeris et inutile ferrumcingi." No, I have outlived the generation with which mutual labors and perils begat mutual confidence and influence. This enterprise is for the young — for those who can follow it up, and bear it through to its consummation.

It shall have all my prayers, and these are the only weapons of an old man. But, in the meantime, are you right in abandoning this property, and your country with it? I think not. My opinion has ever been that, until more can be done for them, we should endeavor; with those whom fortune has thrown on our hands, to feed and clothe them well, protect them from ill usage, require such reasonable labor only as is performed voluntarily by freemen, and be led by no repugnance to abdicate them, and our duties to them. The laws do not permit us to turn them loose, if that were for their good; and to commute them for other property, is to commit them to those whose usage of them we cannot control.

I hope, then, my dear sir, you will reconcile yourself to your country and its unfortunate condition; that you will not lessen its stock of sound disposition, by withdrawing your portion from the mass. That, on the contrary, you will come forward in the public councils, become the missionary of this doctrine, truly Christian, insinuate and inculcate it, softly but steadily, through the medium of writing and conversation, associate others in your labors, and, when the phalanx is formed, bring on and press the proposition perseveringly, until its accomplishment.

It is an encouraging observation that no good measure was ever proposed which, if duly pursued, failed to prevail in the end. We have a proof of this in the history of the endeavors, in the British Parliament, to suppress that very trade which brought this evil on us. And you will be supported by the religious precept, "Be not wearied in well doing." That your success may be as speedy and as complete as it will be honorable and immortal consolation to yourself, I shall as fervently and sincerely pray, as I assure you of my great friendship and respect.

TH. JEFFERSON

BIBLIOGRAPHICAL AIDS

The emphasis in this volume, as in the others in the Presidential Chronology series, is on the administration of the president. But Jefferson was also an astute political theoretician, legal scholar, architect, and highly respected scientist, as well as a radical leader in Virginia and the Continental Congress, governor of Virginia, minister to France, Secretary of State, vice president, and a practical politician who built the first national political party. This bibliography list sources which shed light on these facets of the third president.

So much has been written about Jefferson that this critically selected bibliography cannot include more than a fraction, although it does include the major works. Many other titles can be found in almost any library's card catalog and in some of the works listed here. – Malone has particularly complete listings in his four volumes on Jefferson's life.

For recent articles in scholarly journals, see Reader's Guide to Periodical Literature and Social Science and Humanities Index. For more chronological information, additional relevant documents, and supplementary sources, see the volumes on Washington, Adams, Madison, and Monroe in this series.

Asterisks after titles indicate books available in paperback.

SOURCE MATERIALS

Multi-Volume

the major collection of Jefferson's papers (236 volumes, including documents and letters which he wrote and which were sent to him) is in the Library of Congress. The material has been put on microfilm, which is available in many major libraries. Other materials on his public and private life are in the Coolidge Collection at the Massachussetts Historical Society (67 volumes). The Alderman library at the University of Virginia has an extensive collection of his private papers and supplementary collections of materials by others which give insights into his personal and family life.

Boyd, Julian P., ed. The Papers of Thomas Jefferson. 17 vols. Princeton, 1950-. The first of a projected 50-odd volume series bringing together the letters and other writings by and to Jefferson scattered in repositories all over the nation. The first 17 bring Jefferson up to his last years as ambassador to France.

Cappon, Lester J., ed. The Adams-Jefferson Letters. 2 vols. Chapel
Hill, 1959. Contains the complete correspondence between Jefferson and John and Abigail Adams.

Ford, Paul L., ed. The Writings of Thomas Jefferson. 10 vols. New
York, 1897. Contains letters Jefferson wrote and some to him. Not
complete by any means, bu the most dependable printed collection
prior to Boyd's.

Israel, Fred L., ed. The State of the Union Messages of the Presidents. 1790-1966. 3 vols. New York, 1967. Vol 1 contains all
eight of Jefferson's annual messages in their entirety.

Lipscomb, Andrew A. and Bergh, Albert E., eds. The Writings of
Thomas Jefferson. 20 vols. Washington, 1904. More extensive but
less accurate than Ford's edition.

Single-Volume

Bear, James A., Jr. ed. Jefferson at Monticello. Charlottesville,
1967*. Focuses on his domestic life. Includes memoirs of Isaac,
a slave, and descriptions of Jefferson's family, servants, blooded
stock, manufacturing, appearance, habits, and library. Includes his
will.

Betts, Edwin M. and Bear, James A. Jr., eds. The Family Letters of
Thomas Jefferson. Columbia, 1966. Contains 570 letters between
Jefferson and his daughters and grandchildren from 1783 to his
death in 1826.

Koch, Adrienne and Pedan, William, eds. The Life and Selected Writings of Thomas Jefferson. New York, 1944. Contains a short biography and a wide selection of his letters and papers, public and
private, including extracts from his Autobiography, the Annas,
Notes on Virginia, and travel journals.

Padover, Saul K., ed. A Jefferson Profile. New York, 1956. Contains
180 letters (out of the more than 18,000 Jefferson wrote) which
let him draw a portrait of himself.

BIOGRAPHIES
Multi-Volume

Bowers, Claude G. The Young Jefferson. Boston and New York, 1945;
Jefferson and Hamilton, Boston and New York, 1925; Jefferson in

Power. Boston and New York, 1936. A three-volume biography highly favorable to Jefferson.

Kimball, Marie. Jefferson: the Road to Glory. New York, 1943; Jefferson: War and Peace. New York, 1947; Jefferson: the Scene in Europe. New York, 1950. A curiously flat account of Jefferson's life until his return from France in 1789. More recent titles are more accurate.

Malone, Dumas. Jefferson and His Time, a multi-volume biography, four of which have been published. Jefferson the Virginian. Boston, 1948; Jefferson and the Rights of Man. Boston, 1951; Jefferson and the Ordeal of Liberty. Boston, 1962; Jefferson the President (First Term. 1801-05). Boston 1970. Excellent. Complete, detailed, and authoritative account by a great historian. Volume IV is the first serious study of Jefferson's first term in office since Henry Adams' 10 volume study in 1889 (see "Revolution of 1800" below). Volume V on Jefferson's second term is in preparation. Every published volume contains a detailed chronology and an extensive bibliography.

Randall, Henry S. The Live of Thomas Jefferson. 3 vols. New York, 1858. A thorough portrayal by a man who interviewed some of Jefferson's grandchildren. Some factual errors have been corrected by later scholarship, but the volumes contain many letters and papers, some of which have since been lost.

Schachner, Nathan. Thomas Jefferson. 2 vols. New York, 1951. A consciously iconoclastic portrayal which attempts to show Jefferson, warts and all, and suffers from the limitations of its approach.

Single-Volume

Boorstein, Daniel J. The Lost World of Thomas Jefferson. New York, 1948*. Describes only his ideas, not his life, and the thinking processes of members of the Philadelphia chapter of the American Philosophical Society.

Chinard, Gilbert. Thomas Jefferson: The Apostle of Americanism. rev. ed. Ann Arbor, 1957*. A standard biography.

Fleming, Thomas. The Man from Monticello. New York, 1969. An interesting treatment which tells the story of Jefferson's life from his own point of view.

Nock, Albert J. Jefferson. New York, 1960*. A good short biography.

Padover, Saul K. Jefferson. revised ed. New York, 1952*. Well balanced short biography.

Peterson, Merrill D. Thomas Jefferson and the New Nation. New York, 1970. Focuses on Jefferson's life against the background of his contributions to creation of the United States.

ESSAYS

Andrews, S. "Jefferson and the French Revolution," History Today, 18 (May, 1968), 299-306.

Cardwell, A.G., "Jefferson Renounced: Natural Rights in the Old South," Yale Review, 58 (March, 1969), 388-407.

Cohen, W. "Thomas Jefferson and the Problem of Slavery," Journal of American History, 56 (December, 1969), 503-526.

Fleming, Thomas. "Verdicts of History," American Heritage, 19 (December, 1967), 22-27.

Freidel, F. "Thomas Jefferson, Third President," National Geographic, 126 (November, 1964), 664-671.

Koenig, L.W. "Consensus Politics, 1800-1805." American Heritage, 18 (February, 1967), 4-7.

Malone, Dumas. "Presidential Leaderships and National Unity: The Jeffersonian Example," Journal of Southern History, 35 (February, 1969), 3-17.

————. "Thomas Jefferson." in vol. 10 of the 20-vol. Dictionary of American Biography, New York, 1928-36. The longest of any presidential biography, perhaps because Malone wrote it and was also editor of the entire Dictionary.

Peterson, Merrill D. "Thomas Jefferson and Commercial Policy, 1783-93," William and Mary Quarterly, 22 (October, 1965), 584-610.

————, and Donald, Aida D. eds. Thomas Jefferson: A Profile. New York, 1967.* A collection of essays on Jefferson's beliefs and policies by outstanding scholars.

Steinberg, Alfred. "Thomas Jefferson, the Practical Idealist," Chapter 3, in The First Ten, Garden City, 1967.

MONOGRAPHS AND SPECIAL AREAS

Abernathy, Thomas P. The Burr Conspiracy. New York, 1959. "Oh, what a tangled web we weave, when first we practice to deceive." (Scott)

De Conde, Alexander. The Quasi-War: The Politics and Diplomacy of the Undeclared War with France, 1797-1801. New York, 1966. Perhaps the definitive account of the most important issue during Jefferson's vice presidency.

Hofstadter, Richard. The Idea of a Party System, 1789-1804. Berkeley, 1969.

Kimball, Fisk. Thomas Jefferson: Architect. revised ed. New York, 1968*. A classic.

Levy, Leonard W. Jefferson and Civil Liberties: The Darker Side. Cambridge, 1963. A muckraking account which counterbalances completely positive views of Jefferson.

Martin, Edwin T. Thomas Jefferson: Scientist. New York, 1952*. Catalogs his scientific interests, from astronomy to palentology.

Perkins, Bradford. The First Reapproachment: England and the United States, 1795-1805. Philadelphia, 1955. An important monograph which praises Federalist foreign policy.

Peterson, Merrill D. The Jeffersonian Image in the American Mind. New York, 1960*. Shows how Jefferson's ideas have been used to bolster both sides of many issues and how his image has been created, recreated, interpreted, and misinterpreted.

Sears, Louis M. Jefferson and the Embargo, 1807-1809. Revised ed, Durham, 1960. Describes Jefferson's attitude toward war and international law, the enactment of the embargo, the difficulties in enforcing it, and its repeal.

Smith, James. Freedom's Fetters: The Alien and Sedition Laws and American Civil Liberties. Ithaca, 1956. A definitive work, although some historians challenge Smith's assumption that the Sedition Act was unconstitutional.

Witaker, Arthur P. The Mississippi Question, 1795-1803. New York, 1934. A careful, critical study of one of the most confused chapters in American diplomatic history, which was not settled until the United States took possession of Louisiana.

THE REVOLUTION OF 1800

Adams, Henry. History of the United States of America During the
Administration of Thomas Jefferson. 10 Vols. New York, 1899.
A classic, although written with a pen dipped in acid.

_____ History of the United States During the Administrations of
Jefferson and Madison. Ernst Samuels, ed. Chicago, 1976*. A useful condensation.

Brant, Irving. James Madison: Father of the Constitution (1787-1800).
Vol 3 of a six-vol. biography. New York, 1950.

_____ James Madison: Secretary of State (1801-09). Vol. 4 in the
six-volume biography. New York, 1953.

Cunningham, Noble, E., Jr. The Jeffersonian Republicans: Formation
of Party Organization, 1789-1801. Chapel Hill, 1957.

_____ The Jeffersonian Republicans in Power: Party Operations,
1801-09. Chapel Hill, 1963.

Fischer, David H. The Revolution of American Conservatism: The
Federalist Party in the Era of Jeffersonain Democracy. New York,
1965*. Argues that Federalism did not die out but that younger federalists worked from within the Republican party.

Koch, Adrienne. Jefferson and Madison: The Great Collaboration. New
York, 1950*. A brilliant study of the history of ideas which shows
that Madison was responsible for some ideas Jefferson was credited
with.

White, Leonard D. The Jeffersonians: A Study in Administrative History. New York, 1951. Discusses the administrations of Jefferson,
Madison, Monroe, and John Quincy Adams.

THE PRESIDENCY

Bailey, Thomas A. Presidential Greatness: The Image and the Man
from George Washington to the Present. New York, 1966*. A critical and subjective study of the qualities which comprise presidential greatness. Bailey posits 43 yardsticks for measuring presidents and applies them to every one from Washington through
Lyndon Johnson. He disagrees with both Schlesinger polls (see
below), which place Jefferson fifth in the "Great" category, and
ranks him somewhere in the "Near Great" group.

Binkley, Wildred E. The Man in the White House: His Powers and Duties. Revised ed. New York, 1964. Traces the development of the president's various roles.

Brown, Stuart G. The American Presidency: Leadership, Partisanship, and Popularity. New York, 1966. Likes the more partisan ones like Jefferson and Jackson.

Burns, James M. Presidential Government: The Cruciable of Leadership. New York, 1966. A helpful overview, particularly of the presidency in recent years.

Corwin, Edward S. The President: Office and Powers. 4th ed. New York, 1957. An older classic.

Kane, Joseph N. Facts About the Presidents. New York, 1959. Includes comparative as well as biographical data about the presidents.

Koenig, Louis W. The Chief Executive. New York, 1964. Authoritative study of presidential powers.

Laski, Harold J. The American Presidency. New York, 1964. A classic,

Reedy, George E. The Twilight of the Presidency. New York, 1970. President Johnson's former press secretary argues that the president learns about problems and events only through his advisors and therefore is out of touch with actual situations and the feelings of the American people.

Rossiter, Clinton. The American Presidency, 2nd ed. New York, 1960. Useful.

Schlesinger, Arthur M. Sr. "Historians Rate United States Presidents," Life 25 (November 1, 1948), 65ff.

_____."Our Presidents: A Rating by Seventy-five Historians," New York Times Magazine, July 29, 1962, 12ff.

NAME INDEX